JB JOSSEY-BASS™
A Wiley Brand

Major Gift Essentials

Everything You Need to Know to Secure Big Gifts

Scott C. Stevenson, Editor

WILEY

978-1-118-69160-1   ISBN

978-1-118-70399-1   ISBN (online)

Major Gift Essentials:
Everything You Need to Know To Secure Big Gifts

Published by

Stevenson, Inc.

P.O. Box 4528 • Sioux City, Iowa • 51104

Phone 712.239.3010 • Fax 712.239.2166

www.stevensoninc.com

Major Gift Essentials: Everything You Need to Know to Secure Big Gifts

TABLE OF CONTENTS

TABLE OF CONTENTS

Major Gift Essentials: Everything You Need to Know to Secure Big Gifts

ESTABLISHING A MAJOR GIFTS PROGRAM

Whether your organization is looking to launch its first major gifts program, expand its operations or just solidify its foundation and fundamentals, going back to basics is a critical first step. The principles and strategies found in the following articles will set any major fundraising program on the path to success.

Too Few Prospects? Map Out Plan to Change That

Far too many organizations launch a major fundraising effort without first evaluating whether they have enough capable prospects to get the job done. Then, once a campaign is announced, it becomes clear that they have too few friends capable of giving five-figure-and-above gifts.

If lack of major gift prospects is an issue for your organization, make it a top priority to develop a three- to five-year identification and cultivation plan. That way, when you launch a major fundraising effort, you'll have a pool of capable prospects.

The basic components of that three- to five-year plan should include:

1. Recruiting a board of trustees capable of making five-figure-plus gifts — perhaps a higher minimum depending on your organization's stature and history.

2. Identifying your region's most financially capable individuals, businesses and foundations, which includes prioritizing this group based on research and rating and screening procedures.

3. Developing an ongoing plan of cultivation tailored to each prospect. As a guide, plan on a minimum of six highly individualized cultivation moves before embarking on the solicitation phase.

4. Undertaking a strategic planning process that seeks to involve and engage the identified prospects in various capacities.

Tool Helps Start, Strengthen a Planned Giving Program

Jerold Panas, of Jerold Panas, Linzy & Partners (Chicago, IL), developed a tool specifically to help organizations start a planned giving program or strengthen an existing one.

Shown below, the tool, Coming of Age —The Twenty-One Factors in Designing a Successful Planned Giving Program, is divided into two sections, activity and action.

Even if you have a planned giving program in place, Panas recommends reviewing the steps listed in the tool to make sure your program incorporates all of them. "It is most helpful if you have a consultant who can go through each step and develop ways to put them into practice," he says.

The action section is used to record when activities are completed. "For example, for the first activity, board approval of a planned giving program, you would put the date the board will be meeting to give approval. Each activity has to be time-bonded in order to be effective. If you don't know you have deadlines to meet or hurdles to jump over, there will be no urgency to getting things done."

Source: Jerold Panas, Jerold Panas, Linzy & Partners, Chicago, IL. Phone (312) 222-1212. E-mail: ideas@panaslinzy.com. Website: www.jeroldpanas.com

Content not available in this edition

ESTABLISHING A MAJOR GIFTS PROGRAM

Understand the Science of Determining Funding Priorities

Setting fundraising priorities is a crucial prerequisite to raising major gifts.

Here, Brian Sheridan, development and marketing manager at the Los Angeles and San Gabriel Rivers Watershed Council (Los Angeles, CA), which works to preserve and enhance the watershed's economic and ecological vitality, discusses factors all nonprofits must keep in mind when determining funding priorities:

Is there a one-size-fits-all model for determining funding priorities?

"No. However, there is a one-size-fits-99-percent-of-all-nonprofits model. Board involvement in fundraising and individual donations are key. Individual giving should be emphasized and re-emphasized."

What are some of the key components in any model for determining a nonprofit's fundraising priorities?

"Your model should differentiate between restricted grants and unrestricted sources of funds. In this day of diminishing endowments and tax base, we also have to plan for the eventuality that either of these sources will go down. If we have not diversified, it leaves us with two choices: cut programs or operate in the red. If we have to cut successful programs, then we aren't doing our duty as nonprofits. If we operate in the red, we will only last for so long."

What components should be figured into a nonprofits' model that often are not?

"I think a lot of organizations overlook the value of being included in wills and bequests. I think this is because it is a longer-term payoff, but the benefits can be substantial."

How should a nonprofit determine what kinds of manpower (executive director, board of directors, development director, etc.) will take ownership of its funding priorities?

"Be wary of the development committee or anything else that takes fundraising ownership away from the board. The last thing you want is for the board to say, 'I don't need to fundraise — that's what the development/gala/fundraising/etc. committee is doing.'"

What advice would you give to a nonprofit that is trying to determine what is most needed versus what is most fundable?

"Be careful of chasing the money. When you chase the available funds, you often get a partially funded project, which is expensive to an organization and difficult to pull off. Before you begin budgeting for a program, make sure to have an anchor funder who you are fairly certain will fund the project before going after smaller requests."

Source: Brian Sheridan, Development and Marketing Manager, Los Angeles and San Gabriel Rivers Watershed Council, Los Angeles, CA. Phone (213) 229-9945. E-mail: brian@lasgrwc.org. Website: www.lasgrwc.org

Conduct Financial Assessment of Your Fundraising Programs

One part of creating a yearlong development plan for your organization is conducting a financial assessment of each of your fundraising programs, says Alice L. Ferris, partner at GoalBusters Consulting, LLC (Flagstaff, AZ).

"As much as possible, make sure you can track all the money that comes into your organization for each fundraising program," Ferris says. "For example, you will want to know how much you have raised from special events, annual mailings, advertisements, etc. If you can track it back to the program it originated from, that will help you analyze those programs later in the development of your fundraising plan."

In addition to identifying the revenue from each of your fundraising programs, you will also need to calculate the expenses, says Ferris. She shares two ways to do that:

1. **Calculate your expenses based on true net.** The true net of an event or program includes two additional things that organizations don't always accommodate for, she says. They are 1) how much staff time it takes, and 2) how much volunteer time it takes. "When we calculated the true net for one organization that conducted an annual four-day event held over a holiday, they ended up netting somewhere in the neighborhood of $6,000 to $10,000 for the event," she says.

2. **Benchmark your expenses against other programs.** Some sectors have benchmarks you can compare yourself against, but if you don't have a benchmarking tool in your nonprofit area, Ferris recommends dividing revenue by individual giving, planned giving, foundation giving and corporate giving, then determining what percentage of your revenue comes from each area. "For instance, some organizations are going to have a huge percentage of revenue coming from foundations," she says. "Others will have a large percentage of revenue coming from corporate support."

What you're looking for, says Ferris, is whether your percentages line up with the GivingUSA statistics.

"GivingUSA (www.givingusa.org) of Glenview, IL, tracks charitable giving in the USA in four areas — individual, corporate, bequests and foundations," says Ferris. "You want 75 percent, or at least the majority of your contributions, to be from individuals. Individuals are going to be your most stable source of renewable income. If they aren't right now, that will give you an opportunity to plan for the future and try to move things toward that 75 percent."

Source: Alice L. Ferris, Partner, GoalBusters Consulting, LLC, Flagstaff, AZ. Phone (928) 606-1692. E-mail: alice.ferris@goalbusters.net

ESTABLISHING A MAJOR GIFTS PROGRAM

Break Lofty Goals Into Achievable Parts

When it comes to raising major gifts, lofty goals can be debilitating if you let them overwhelm you. That's why it's critical you break goals down into achievable and sequential steps.

How you break those goals down is equally important. Get rid of should goals and focus on what makes achieving them more energizing for you personally. Beyond goal setting and creating a time line in which to achieve those goals, split your overall time frame into months, weeks and even days. "What will I need to accomplish on a monthly basis, on a weekly basis and each day?"

For your daily to-do list, prioritize what three to five things you need to accomplish that day, since that's all most people can handle with thoroughness and competence.

As you progress through each week, be accountable, not only to your supervisor but to yourself. Did you meet that week's objectives? Where did you fall short? Why? What behaviors will you change this week and in the weeks ahead to make up for it?

Create a personal plan for achieving your goals by breaking them down into bite-sized pieces, prioritizing them, sequencing them and tackling them with confidence and enthusiasm. Use the example below to craft one that works for you.

Personal Goal: Raise $2 million in 2011

To make that happen:

✓ Solicit no less than 70 probable donors for gifts of $50,000 to $2 million.

✓ Make, on average, five cultivation/solicitation contacts with each probable donor throughout 2011, recognizing that 350 total contacts per year equates to 30 meaningful contacts per month or 1.5 contacts per day.

Jumpstart Major Giving With a Wealth Sweep

A $10,000 investment in a wealth sweep is paying back exponentially for Clemson University (Clemson, SC), says Bobby Couch, executive director of major gifts.

"Our wealth sweep generated well in excess of $2 million in new money," Couch says. "And we've only begun to scratch the surface."

The sweep began when development staff submitted 55,000 names from a donor database and athletic ticket database to prospect research firm Wealth Engine (Bethesda, MD). Couch says they then sliced and diced the resulting reams of data to create a workable list of 3,500 persons capable of $100,000-plus gifts. The list included both those who appeared in university databases but were unknown to development staff, and long-term supporters of the program who had not been approached for a major gift.

The results were eye-opening, he says. "People we'd never have guessed turned out to have the capacity to give at significant levels of support. And some we didn't know at all."

They divided the 3,500 names into geographic markets and financial capacity. Given the volume of names, staff had their hands full just approaching the $1 million-plus category. Couch estimates that only around 10 percent of the 3,500 have been contacted.

Couch says conducting wealth sweeps every three to five years is ideal, but estimates that data could serve seven to 10 years. He also recommends a frank assessment of internal resources before undertaking such a venture. "If you do not have the staff to support the results, the data will just sit on a shelf and you will not get a return of your investment," he says, noting that his development staff has doubled since its first sweep five years ago, and is still expanding.

Source: Bobby Couch, Executive Director of Major Gifts, Clemson University Athletics/IPTAY, Clemson, SC. Phone (864) 656-0361. E-mail: Jcouch@clemson.edu

Ten Questions Prospect Management Systems Should Answer

Is your prospect management system ensuring that the right solicitor asks the right prospect for the right amount supporting the right program at the right time? Or are you just recording contact reports, asks Christina Pulawski, principle of Christina Pulawski Consulting (Chicago, IL).

Pulawski says a prospect management system is not a way to measure things — contacts, visits, etc. — but rather "a system of managing the identification, cultivation, solicitation and stewardship of prospective donors through strategic actions designed to move each prospect toward the fullest possible relationship with your organization."

Pulawski says a management system should be able to answer specific, practical questions such as:

1. How many prospects are in the solicitation pipeline?
2. How many major gifts are being solicited or planned?
3. How many of those solicitations are successful? What is our yield?
4. How many prospects have been identified for specific projects?
5. What proportion of dollars is actually being raised through development efforts?
6. How much revenue can be projected for a year or campaign?
7. How are staff performing against goals?
8. What activities are most effective with different types of prospects?
9. Are there enough prospects to meet organizational needs?
10. Are quality major gift prospects being neglected?

Source: Christina Pulawski, Principle, Christina Pulawski Consulting, Chicago, IL. Phone (773) 255-3873. E-mail: c-pulawski@comcast.net

ESTABLISHING A MAJOR GIFTS PROGRAM

Goal-setting Road Map Points the Way to Increased Revenue

In one fiscal year, OSF Saint Francis/Children's Hospital of Illinois Foundation (Peoria, IL) increased major gifts and planned giving by an impressive 70 percent.

Andrew Schuster, senior development director, credits the increase to highly organized long-term goal planning. He shares 11 steps to goal planning for development success:

1. Organization goals are set for the year based on core mission, vision and values.
2. Department management reviews organization goals and department long-term strategic plan with staff to create annual department priorities as they relate to overall organization goals.
3. Each person in the department creates individual goals and priorities to support the department strategic plan and annual priorities. This process is based on roles and responsibilities within the department. Everything should be in writing.
4. All staff come together to share feedback on priorities and goals.
5. Key questions include: Are the priorities consistent with the mission, vision and values of the organization? Are the priorities aligned with the strategic plan?
6. Key goals are selected for each area in the department. Not all goals will be a priority for the year.
7. The manager works with each staff person to create individual objectives that support department annual priorities.
8. Create an action plan to help achieve department annual priorities for each person.
9. Submit annual priorities to executive for approval.
10. Execute the plan!
11. Review annual priorities quarterly. Make adjustments as necessary. Understand that annual priorities are different than annual goals. Priorities refer to the departments' overall strategic plan and focus for the year. Goals refer to individual goals and department goals that will help obtain annual priorities.

Source: Andrew Schuster, Senior Development Director, OSF Saint Francis/Children's Hospital of Illinois Foundation, Peoria, IL. Phone (309) 566-5666. E-mail: Andrew.Schuster@osfhealthcare.org

Benefits of Team Goal Planning

A 70 percent increase in major gifts and planned giving is just one benefit OSF Saint Francis/Children's Hospital of Illinois Foundation (Peoria, IL) reaped with long-term goal planning. Andrew Schuster, senior development director, says a concrete planning process can also help organizations by:

✓ Helping create a system that moves donors along the donor continuum.

✓ Allowing each staff member to understand how events, major gifts, planned giving and donor relations relate to one another.

✓ Giving all staff a better understanding of how each area supports the others and how important it is to communicate often regarding various aspects of an event and/or cultivation of a prospective donor.

✓ Creating buy-in from all staff. If everyone participates in the process and has a chance to create goals and offer feedback, the staff becomes invested.

Put Firm Numbers on Major Gift Solicitation

Outstanding fundraising comes not from guesswork but from hard data that goes back to the earliest stages of the solicitation process, says Christina Pulawski, principal of Christina Pulawski Consulting (Chicago, IL).

Pulawski says systematic and reliable fundraising includes understanding and calculating your organization's prospect yield — the percentage of solicited prospects who donate at the level you suggest.

Imagine you have 20 promising prospects identified, she says. Of these, you might be successful in approaching only 16 of them. Of these 16, you may qualify only 12 as having sufficient capacity and interest in your cause. Of the 12, you may succeed in actively cultivating only eight. Of the eight, cultivation might proceed far enough to solicit only four of them. And of those four, only one might say yes to the amount you request. Your average yield, then, is one out of 20, or 5 percent.

Yield is a valuable metric in itself, but it can also be used to enhance major gift forecasting. Multiplying the total number of proposals planned over a certain period by the fundraising process (the yield of prospects qualified from the total, etc.) will aid in understanding where your processes may be able to be improved, or where more or better information may be needed, says Pulawski.

Yield is a valuable metric in itself, but it can also be used to enhance major gift forecasting. Multiplying the total number of proposals planned over a certain period of time by rate prospects are actually solicited by your organization, the solicitation yield and the average dollar amount of major gifts gives a reliable estimate of the revenue you can realistically expect to generate:

(planned proposals) x (solicitation rate) x (yield) x (avg. gift) = (total projected commitments)

Pulawski says it's important to remember that at least six months to a year's worth of accurate data are often needed to generate remotely reliable projections.

Source: Christina Pulawski, Principal, Christina Pulawski Consulting, Chicago, IL. Phone (773) 255-3873. E-mail: c-pulawski@comcast.net

ESTABLISHING A MAJOR GIFTS PROGRAM

When Developing Yearlong Fundraising Plan, Conduct a SWOT Analysis

When developing a yearlong fundraising plan, be sure to analyze any previously developed fundraising plans, say James Anderson, partner at GoalBusters Consulting, LLC (Flagstaff, AZ). One way to do so is a SWOT analysis, in which you look at your organization's strengths, weaknesses, opportunities and threats.

Anderson outlines what to look for when analyzing each area:

Strengths (internal): What do you do well or exceptionally? What unique value do you offer? What are the things you want to keep doing and that you can do better than other organizations?

Weaknesses (internal): What are the things you know you are not doing well? Are there things you need to change because it feels as though you just keep pounding your head against the wall? Or are they things you simply don't do well either because you don't know how or don't have the resources to do properly?

Opportunities (external): What could you be doing or doing more of? Where could you extend your offerings, services and programs? Where could you potentially tap donors and donor bases that you may be currently overlooking or not fully capitalizing on?

Threats (external): What things have the potential to negatively impact your plan and your organization? When you identify a threat, one way to assess it is to ask what the worst-case scenario is. Some examples of external threats: 1) You are heavily grant-funded, and funds are going to dry up, 2) You are heavily funded by a foundation and investments aren't returning as strong as they used to, and you know that will negatively impact gifts. "When assessing threats, you'll be facing either conditions or problems," he says. "Conditions are things you may have to address or handle but you have no real control over. However, problems are something which you can solve, resolve or fix."

When looking at your SWOT findings, Anderson says, watch for intersections of the areas and respond as follows:

- ❑ **Where strengths and opportunities intersect, invest.** You want to invest more of your resources, time and capital on these opportunities.

- ❑ **Where weaknesses and threats intersect,** consider divesting yourself of that project or program, unless it is something you truly must maintain.

- ❑ **Where strengths and threats intersect, defend.** "If you have an external threat to one of your strengths, don't let that negatively impact something that you do well," he says. "Instead, analyze what that situation is and determine how you can best continue to capitalize on that strength."

- ❑ **Where weaknesses and opportunities intersect, identify areas for improvement.** "It may be a situation in which you can bolster the area of weakness or capitalize on what the opportunity is with the investment of additional resources, but that is a decision where you will have to look at whether your internal resources will allow it, and whether the return on investment is worth the commitment of the additional resources," he says.

Sources: James Anderson, Partner, GoalBusters Consulting, LLC, Flagstaff, AZ. Phone (928) 890-8239. E-mail: jim.anderson@goalbusters.net

---

A Look at the Creation of a Strategic Plan

Southern Illinois University-Carbondale Foundation (Carbondale, IL) underwent a 10-month process in developing its four-year strategic plan (2009-2012).

At the May meeting, the board, with the assistance of a consultant-facilitator, participated in a brainstorming session to identify five broad strategic categories, says Rickey N. McCurry, vice chancellor for institutional advancement at Southern Illinois University and chief executive officer of the foundation.

The foundation board then convened a task force of five to six board members headed by the foundation board's immediate past president and board officers.

Over the next six months, members of the task force were divided up, given a leader and put in charge of conducting a SWOT analysis (Strengths, Weaknesses, Opportunities and Threats) on each of the five strategic categories, which they did through teleconference meetings, he says.

At the foundation board's October meeting, each task force leader presented to the full board results of the SWOT analysis, and the board members either affirmed or adjusted what was presented. The groups then took that feedback, refined it and developed goals, says McCurry.

In February, the entire foundation board convened at a two-day off-campus board retreat to work on the opportunities and goals for each of the strategic categories.

From that meeting, McMurry and the task force chair wrote the final draft of the strategic plan, which provided specific wording for each strategic category.

The foundation began the strategic planning process as it was coming to the conclusion of its first-ever comprehensive capital campaign, McCurry notes. "We felt it was important to engage in a strategic planning process at that time because we wanted to assess where we were, where we needed to go, and how to get there," he says. "A major purpose and goal in developing the strategic plan was to launch our next campaign. One of our major focal areas in our strategic plan is resource generation and under that is fundraising and the next campaign, which will have a goal between $250 million and $500 million."

While the strategic plan serves as the blueprint to follow over the four year period, it also must be flexible as well, says McCurry: "It is our philosophy and strong belief that good plans have inherent flexibility built in. The value of a good plan is shown by providing a solid foundation and framework on which to build — and from which to adapt as real need and situations dictate."

Source: Rickey N. McCurry, Vice Chancellor for Institutional Advancement and Chief Executive Officer, Southern Illinois University-Carbondale, Carbondale, IL. Phone (618) 453-4900. E-mail: mccurry@siu.edu

ESTABLISHING A MAJOR GIFTS PROGRAM

What's Your Restricted Gifts Policy?

Creating wide-reaching, appropriate policies allows you to always be ready to act when your major gifts pursuits result in significant gifts.

At the New Hampshire Historical Society (Concord, NH), staff developed gift acceptance policies to help focus support on the most important aspects of their mission, says Anne L. Hamilton, director of development.

"A policy outlining the acceptance of restricted gifts lets prospective donors know that we welcome these types of gifts in mission-related core areas," she says. "It also lets them know that there is a significant amount of time involved in maintaining and tracking separately endowed funds, as well as the reasoning behind requiring a minimum amount to establish a restricted endowment."

The society's restricted gifts policy lists the following conditions under which restricted gifts will be accepted:

- Must be compatible with the overall mission of the society.

- Shall not impede the ability of the society to acquire gifts from other sources.

- Shall not place undue burden on the society's resources.

- Shall not subject the society to adverse publicity.

Donors can either restrict their gifts to a current endowment fund or create their own restricted endowment fund with a minimum gift of $100,000.

"The benchmark of $100,000 for a restricted gift pays out enough money annually to make a difference," says Hamilton. "We currently have a number of named restricted funds that were accepted prior to the adoption of our restricted funds policy that do not meet the $100,000 minimum. Often we let those funds sit over a number of years until we have enough growth in available payout funds to make a difference or to purchase something important."

The society's restricted gifts policy also requires restricted gift donors to sign a gift agreement describing the use of the funds, avoiding unreasonable limitations or restrictions, and providing a clause giving the society the flexibility to use the funds for a similar purpose if the original use is no longer possible or practical.

One example of a restricted gift that fits within the society's restricted gifts policy is an estate gift made by Bryant Tolles. Tolles left the society his collection of White Mountains memorabilia and an endowment to care for the items in perpetuity and to purchase new items for the collection.

"Not only did he give us his whole collection of items of great interest to New Hampshire, but he gave us a sizable endowment to support it, which fits the criteria laid out in our restricted gifts policy," says Hamilton. "His gift will significantly enhance what we already have in our collection. Not only will his endowment allow us to care for his pieces, but also purchase other items related to the White Mountains to add to the collection."

Source: Anne L. Hamilton, Director of Development, New Hampshire Historical Society, Concord, NH. Phone (603) 228-6688. E-mail: ahamilton@nhhistory.org

Craft Policies to Address Gifts of Personal Property

Gifts of jewelry, works of art, antiques, special collections, rare books and manuscripts can bring prestige and one-of-a-kind value to nonprofits. But gifts of personal property are far less flexible than cash, and nonprofit representatives must be careful to make sure such gifts do not drain more resources than they provide.

These points, developed by staff at Antioch University New England (AUNE), Keene, NH, address issues vital to the framework of gift acceptance policies:

- Personal property and real estate gifts cannot require AUNE's commitment to a significant additional expense for present or future use, display, maintenance, administration or sale.

- Donors must demonstrate proof of sole ownership.

- AUNE's acceptance also takes into consideration the usefulness of the item as it pertains to the AUNE's mission and purpose.

Source: Antioch University New England, Keene, NH. Phone (800) 553-8920. Website: http://www.antiochne.edu/giving/property.cfm

Major Gift Essentials: Everything You Need to Know to Secure Big Gifts

IDENTIFYING TOP-DOLLAR PROSPECTS

Few aspects of fundraising are more challenging than identifying new major gift prospects. Numerous nonprofits struggle in this critical area, but a few experience-tested solutions can make all the difference. Assessment tools, research strategies and approaches to prospect and wealth screening are among the tools covered in the following pages.

Methods for Assessing a Donor's Giving Potential

The ability to determine a person's net worth for the purposes of fundraising is a myth that has been perpetuated for years. Even if you know the majority of a person's assets, you most likely will not know all of his or her liabilities. And you have to know both to know the net worth.

That doesn't mean you can't estimate an individual's raw capability to donate. There are a number of formulas and guides available for this purpose, and trial and error may be needed to figure out the best one for your constituents.

Following is a sampling of some of the more popular assessment methods, including some hypothetical examples, illustrated at left. Just remember, you still have to convince the person to give to your cause.

In seeking to assess a donor's giving potential, keep in mind:

1. Liquidity is key, unless you are looking for donations of property. Even stock holdings may not be available for donations in certain circumstances.

2. Annual gifts are generally based on income and capital gifts are based on assets.

3. Consider age, number and ages of children, lifestyle and cost of living for the location.

4. Only stock holdings for insiders and owners of 5 percent and above are reported and available as public information.

5. Assets held in trusts are difficult to find through research.

6. Information on executives and directors of public companies is more available. Proxy statements can be very helpful in identifying income, stock holdings, retirement plans and other indications of wealth.

7. Those in real estate and agriculture are often land-rich and cash-poor.

8. Owners of private companies may be putting all of their earnings back into the company. On the other hand, they may be getting additional perks from this affiliation, such as home allowances, cars, paid vacations, etc., that would offset usual living expenses and leave them with more liquidity.

9. The ownership of valuable property can be expensive to maintain. This includes lavish homes, ranches, art collections, cars, boats, etc. Consider property taxes, insurance, hired staff, and other costs as liabilities when figuring assets and worth. Remember that assessed value may have no relationship to purchase price or market value.

10. Stock brokers and investors usually have a higher proportion of their wealth in stocks and bonds. Venture capitalists generally have more cash, but it may be tied up in investments.

11. Income estimates are available for many professions in several sources.

12. Ratings and net worth estimates are available from several electronic screening vendors. Ask how they arrive at their figures before using the data.

Methods & Formulas To Determine Wealth

- *Stanley and Danko's The Millionaire Next Door —*

  Age times Income divided by 10 = Net Worth

  Example: 50-year-old with annual income from all sources of $200,000 has a net worth of $1 million.

- *IRS (determined from estates with net worth of $600,000+)*

  Male Top Wealthholders

Closely Held Stock	=	14.3% of Net Worth
Other Stock	=	15.2% of Net Worth
Personal Residence	=	8.8% of Net Worth
Other Real Estate	=	15.8% of Net Worth
Other Assets	=	27.9% of Net Worth
Retirement Assets	=	12.7% of Net Worth
Cash/Money Markets	=	5.3% of Net Worth

  Examples:
  Residence valued at $200,000/0.088 = $2,272,727
  Corporate Stock holdings of $200,000/0.152 = $1,315,789

  Female Top Wealthholders

Closely Held Stock	=	6.2% of Net Worth
Other Stock	=	20.5% of Net Worth
Personal Residence	=	11.2% of Net Worth
Other Real Estate	=	15.4% of Net Worth
Other Assets	=	33.2% of Net Worth
Retirement Assets	=	6.4% of Net Worth
Cash/Money Markets	=	7.1% of Net Worth

  Examples:
  Residence valued at $200,000/0.112 = $1,785,714
  Corporate Stock holdings of $200,000/0.205 = $975,610

- *Other Formulas*

  A. 10% of annual income = 5-year giving ability
  B. 1% of liquid assets = 5-year giving ability
  C. 5% of total known assets = 5-year giving ability
  D. 20 x level of consistent annual giving = 5-year giving ability
  E. 10 x annual income = net worth; appropriate ask amount for a gift over 5 years is 5% of net worth

---

IDENTIFYING TOP-DOLLAR PROSPECTS

Take a Four-sided Approach to Prospect Identification

Identifying prospects may feel like looking for a needle in a haystack. Many organizations have entire research teams dedicated to the task; others rely largely on the luck of the draw. Whatever your organization's size or capacity, here are four lenses experts in the philanthropic fundraising field agree will help you to identify prospects who will make worthwhile additions to your donor pool:

1. **Financial viability.** It's not enough to know a donor is wealthy. In today's economy, it's important to know what type of wealth your prospect has. A little bit of research and time with a calculator can tell you a donor's approximate financial worth: work history can guide you to approximate salary, while a home address can give you an idea of property value. Even resources such as family obituaries can help you understand how much a donor's family may have. How does the prospect spend leisure time? Does he/she have stocks? How are those stocks doing? Gauge giving capacity by looking at past philanthropy to other organizations. By simply combing public records, you can educate your gift officers as to the realistic feasibility of a gift. This keeps you from wasting the time and resources of both you and your prospect.

2. **Connection to your organization.** For many gift officers, organizational affiliation is the first step in connecting with a potential donor. Experts say that merely relying on your organization's reach can limit your scope. By exploring a potential prospect's background, you may unearth a less obvious connection to your organization or your organization's mission: Maybe she took a summer program at your university as a child; maybe he has a grandchild with the same learning disability for which your organization has developed a new treatment. However small the connection may seem initially, it could be the key to a long-lasting and lucrative relationship with a new donor. You won't know the depth of that connection until you plumb it.

3. **Philanthropy.** As mentioned above, a donor's philanthropic activity can offer clues to financial solvency. Past giving can also help identify something more difficult to quantify: a donor's interest in helping others, and the way(s) in which he/she goes about doing so. Just because a donor gives to an organization similar to yours doesn't mean he/she wouldn't also be interested in giving to your cause. Or maybe your organization offers something (a research focus or aspect of patient care, for example) that the donor's current charity does not. The same argument holds true if the prospect gives to organizations with very different missions than your own. Just because they support such causes doesn't mean they'll say no to your request.

4. **Demographic.** Persons with the capacity to give may be more or less likely to do so depending on where they are in their lives and careers. For instance, if your organization engages in cutting-edge or experimental research, you may have more success attracting younger donors more willing to invest in such an untested effort than retired donors, who may prefer giving to well-known organizations rooted in tradition. It is a more efficient use of your fundraisers' energy to match donors with projects more likely to meet their social and financial demographic.

Inclination to Give Is Part of Research Equation

Important as it is to identify and measure a prospect's financial capability, it's also important to gauge a prospect's inclination to give. Whether you're meeting with a focus group or steering committee or confining your research to staff, categorizing perceptions about an individual's inclination to give helps prioritize prospects and determine cultivation steps and timing for eventual solicitation.

Examples of inclination levels you can use as a tool include:

❑ **High inclination** — More than likely this individual has already given generously in the past and has an obvious linkage to your organization (e.g., board member, donor, regular patron). He/she may be highly involved with your organization in some capacity.

❑ **Above-average inclination** — The individual has some degree of linkage to the organization and may or may not have contributed in the past.

❑ **Average inclination** — Although the individual may appear favorably disposed to the organization, there is no history to indicate he/she has any ties or interest. He/she may have been supportive of other philanthropic causes.

❑ **Below-average inclination** — Some past action (e.g., a past development call, something that was said by the prospect) indicates that the prospect may look unfavorably upon the organization even though he/she has supported other causes.

❑ **Little or no inclination** — The individual has no interest in the organization and little or no history of past support to other charitable causes.

IDENTIFYING TOP-DOLLAR PROSPECTS

Tips to Maximize Your Prospect Screening Sessions

Are you planning prospect rating and screening sessions among board members, donors and friends of your organization? Maximize the results by incorporating these tips:

- Develop a planning time line by beginning with the screening session date and working backward.

- Segment who screens various prospect groups: those in the same profession as the screener; those with similar philanthropic interests as the screener; those who reside in the same geographic area as those being screened.

- Limit the sessions to two hours or less to respect participants' time, then be sure to start and stop on time.

- Hold sessions at locations that are the most easily accessible for the majority of attendees and perhaps hold some drawing-card appeal (e.g. the exclusive home of a board member).

Don't Overlook the Obvious When Seeking Major Gift Prospects

Seeking to identify major gift prospects or to launch a major capital campaign? Pay attention to those who faithfully show up for your events. You may be overlooking potential right under your nose.

One Midwest high school, for example, had a single man who attended every event it sponsored, yet no one approached him for support. The man died with no will and an estate in excess of $3 million.

Ask Your Major Donors for a Referral

Want to realize more major gifts? Ask your major donors to refer you to others who might have an interest in supporting your organization, says Jean Block, president of Jean Block Consulting, Inc. (Albuquerque, NM), "Ask them, 'Now that you know who we are and what we're about, whom do you think we should contact?'"

Source: Jean Block, President, Jean Block Consulting, Inc., Albuquerque, NM. Phone (505) 899-1520. E-mail: jean@blockinc.com

Assessing Donor Giving Preferences

 How do you determine which donors would be more drawn to endowment gifts, as opposed to those who would prefer capital projects?

"At the industry level, there is a pendulum that swings back and forth between different funding options. Several years ago, everyone wanted bricks and mortar, and endowment was almost a dirty word. Now donors seem to be feeling that financial strength is as important as physical presence. Research on past giving is of course crucial, but we find many major donors are quite open to being sold. Individuals might have supported major construction projects in the past, but if an organization they love has other priorities — and that organization can clearly articulate those priorities — they will often go along with it."

— *Robert Evans, Founder and Managing Director, The EHL Consulting Group, Inc. (Willow Grove, PA)*

"Probing donors' priorities and then really listening is key. Say a donor says they want to leave a legacy that would benefit students. Exploring that further, they might say that the only way they went to college was on somebody's scholarship and they want to provide that support to future generations. That obviously suggests an endowment. But maybe they instead talk about how the best way to assist students is to provide top-notch facilities and a world-class learning environment. This would lead to a discussion of capital options. It always comes

back to, 'Talk to us a bit more about that.'"

— *Jerome Davies, Senior Vice President for Development, KU Endowment, University of Kansas (Lawrence, KS)*

"It really depends on specifics — what the endowment is for and what the capital campaign components are directed at — but in a bad economy, returns on investments are so abysmal that people tend to shy away from endowments. They worry that the endowment could go underwater and are therefore much more hesitant than when returns were at 12 or 15 percent. It's always important to take wider economic circumstances into consideration."

— *Alton Whitt, Assistant Vice President for Development, University of Alabama at Birmingham Development Office (Birmingham, AL)*

"One major determinant we use is donors' length and history of giving. We have donors who have been making regular gifts for 20 to 30 years, and many of these tend to value gifts that continue into perpetuity. These long-term, often older donors are frequently looking toward the future quality of programs and, in my experience, tend to prefer endowments over capital campaigns, even if they have the resources to make a large one-time gift."

— *Kevin Hughes, Director of Gift Planning, Children's Hospital & Research Center Foundation (Oakland, CA)*

IDENTIFYING TOP-DOLLAR PROSPECTS

Mine Your Existing Database for Major Donors, Prospects

Since the key to building a major donor program is creating and maintaining relationships, look first to your database of supporters for potential major gifts, says Sandra G. Ehrlich, director of fund development services at Zielinski Companies (St. Louis, MO).

According to industry statistics, approximately 4 to 5 percent of the current donors in your database have the ability to make a major gift, says Ehrlich. For example, if your database contains 5,000 names, it should contain 150 to 200 potential major donors.

"Use your database to determine how many individuals are giving at a significant level," she says. "Begin by running a report of donors who have made a $1,000 single gift. If you find 10,000 donors, you'll need to revise your criteria. If you find 100, you are in the ballpark. If you find only two, drop the baseline to $500 and go from there."

After determining your baseline and criteria for a major donor, separate major donors and prospects into meaningful and manageable segments, she says, "Zielinski Companies recommends creating tiers of major donors and prospects to care for each donor as personally as you can, while staying focused on those donors who will likely give the majority of funds in any given campaign or year."

Tier 1 donors are your top donors who rate high in capability and willingness in a consistent and strategic manner.

Tier 2 donors may be high in capacity or willingness, but likely not both.

Tier 3 prospects are those with whom you have some connection and are known to have capacity, but haven't yet developed a deep knowledge of or interest in your organization.

Rank your major donors on their proximity to the gift, says Ehrlich, by asking:

- How close are they to giving?
- Have you been in touch with them recently?
- Have they been in touch with you recently?
- Have they hinted or stated that an outright gift might be coming?
- Do you know them well enough?
- Do you feel comfortable that you might receive a gift on the next call?

"Major donors are often rated initially on a two-part scale: willingness and capability," she says. "Willingness refers to a donor's connection to your organization and his or her level of interest and commitment to support the difference you are making in the community. Capability refers to a donor's financial capacity to support your organization."

Once you finish ranking your major donors, consider the capacity of your staff to manage those prospects, says Ehrlich:

"A full-time major gifts officer can likely handle between 50 and 100 of your Tier 1 donors. Another 200 to 300 donors may fit into the Tier 2 segment. When functioning optimally, your nonprofit will be in touch in a meaningful way with all three tiers at least once a month. For Tier 1 donors and prospects, you'll need to create individualized strategies based on your knowledge of those individuals. For Tiers 2 and 3, you'll create group strategies that are as personalized as possible."

Source: Sandra G. Ehrlich, Director, Fund Development Services, Zielinski Companies, St. Louis, MO. Phone (800) 489-2150. E-mail: sehrlich@zielinskico.com. Website: www.zielinskico.com

Identify, Prioritize Funders

Maureen Martin, senior director of foundation relations for the University of Michigan (Ann Arbor, MI), answers some questions about how they identify and prioritize foundation funders:

What steps do you go through to identify and then prioritize your most likely foundation supporters?

"As in any kind of fundraising, our best prospects for future support are our current and recent donors. So we begin there, watching for whether any foundations have decreased or halted their giving across time, whether there's been a change in pattern of giving or in staffing. Then we watch closely any and all foundations that are active in our region — either within the state or the larger multi-state region. Finally, we peruse the databases of foundation grants and foundation news items for tips on major funding initiatives from elsewhere in the country. We prioritize by a combination of likelihood of success and size of potential gift/grant."

How do you identify funders in the first place, and then once you do, how do you go about prioritizing them based on importance/likelihood of a gift?

"We do as tight a read as possible of past grants, grant guidelines and programs, etc. So we undertake a deep review of the grants path of the foundation (for example, we can see whether the foundation gives grants nationally or has a few areas of focus, gives a lot or a few grants at scale, has ever funded in our home state, funds in areas in which we are particularly strong, etc.), and then work with faculty to understand if our work correlates to the foundation areas of interest/support. Our regional donor prospects will always have the deepest review; then the larger but more geographically remote prospects will receive less frequent but thorough review perhaps three or four times a year."

Source: Maureen Martin, Senior Director, Foundation Relations, University of Michigan, Ann Arbor, MI. Phone (734) 647-6074. E-mail: martinms@umich.edu

IDENTIFYING TOP-DOLLAR PROSPECTS

Electronic Toolkits Help to Identify Property

How important is the process of identifying property holdings in major prospect research? Hugely important, says Laura Solla, founder of Research & Development Strategies (Freeport, PA) and author of two books on the subject.

Solla shares some expertise on this critical aspect of the fundraising process.

Why is property so important to prospect research?

"Several reasons, Real estate is one of the few assets almost everybody owns. It is fairly easy to trace, even for a novice. And it gives a good indication of a prospect's overall potential."

Where should one start when conducting property research?

"If you have a particular address you're interested in, it's quite simple. Here are a few websites I recommend.

✓ "Zillow.com will give a valuation based on public record characteristics of a property. It is a great way to determine sellable value which is always preferable to assessed or market value.

✓ "Cyberhomes.com and ZipRealty.com are similar to Zillow, and provide different source options to compare values."

What if you don't have an address?

"The data broker services Intelius.com and KnowX.com area great people-finder tools. For $2, you can enter a person's name and get primary address information along with age, phone number and other individuals living at the address. Keep in mind, however, that to effectively analyze overall wealth, the summer home in Maine or the vacation home in Florida is just as important as the primary residence."

What are some of the higher-end research tools?

"For organizations doing a lot of prospect research I recommend a subscription to Wealthengine.com, Donorsearch. net or Researchpoint from Blackbaud. Costing $1,500 to $3,000 a year, these subscriptions provide access to a real estate finder capable of identifying multiple addresses for the same prospect. They will also give access to databases indicating things like corporate affiliations, board affiliations and charitable giving."

With so many online services, is there any need to go to the assessor's office anymore?

"Rarely, many counties now offer free online real-estate record searches. The only reason I see to actually drive down to city hall or the courthouse is if your geographic focus is local, you have several prospects to research, and your county does not offer an online record search. Aside from that, you can just do it from your office computer."

Contact: Laura Solla, Founder, Prospect Research & Development Strategies. Freeport, PA. Phone (724) 295-0679. E-mail: Solla@ResearchProspects.com. Website: www.ResearchProspects.com

Research Source of Wealth When Measuring Giving Capacity

Giving capacity is arguably the most important factor in prospect identification. But closely linked to giving capacity is another important and often-overlooked aspect of donor research — the source of a donor's wealth.

Gleaning whether prospects have the funds they have promised, and that those funds are not ill-gotten, is a critical step in prospect identification.

The system of vetting potential donors is not elaborate; it is just an extension of the prospect research system which your organization should already have in place, says David Lamb, senior consultant, Target Analytics (Parker, CO). "When you think about giving capacity," Lamb says, "you are already thinking about the source of the wealth."

Poonam Prasad, founder and president, Prasad Consulting & Research (New York, NY) calls this process due diligence. "Your research and donor relation teams should already know about prospects before ever speaking with them," Prasad says, "what their interests are, their business history, financial history, giving history. This is the same thing."

But Prasad warns that excitement for a large donation can often trump due diligence. She cites a case of a major state university that announced a $1 million gift, which later proved to be an empty promise.

In other cases, Lamb says, "Organizations learn that a donor obtained funds in a way that was antithetical to their values. It can cause a great deal of embarrassment."

In such cases, the problem lies largely in a communication disconnect. The research team may notice something amiss and not inform the donor relations team; the donor relations team may enter into a conversation with a potential donor without first asking the research team to vet him or her. For this reason, it is essential to keep all development team members aware of each other's actions.

Lamb suggests pre-empting the issue of gift source by writing gift policies: to decide ahead of time what kind of gifts the institution is willing to accept and which it is not.

In the same vein, be sure to share any discrepancies in a donor's history among departments. "If a donor has been giving at the $1,000 level and then suddenly gives $2 million, you may want to ask why," says Prasad. Donors should have transparent financial histories, with visible patterns. If something doesn't add up, speak up.

Sources: David Lamb, Senior Consultant, Target Analytics: A Blackbaud Company, Parker, CO. Phone (843) 216-6200. E-mail: david.lamb@blackbaud.com. Website: www.blackbaud.com/targetanalytics/overview.aspx Poonam Prasad, Founder and President, Prasad Consulting & Research, New York, NY. Phone (212) 755-1309. E-mail: poonam@prasadconsulting.com. Website: prasadconsulting.com

Major Gift Essentials: Everything You Need to Know to Secure Big Gifts

CULTIVATING MAJOR DONORS

It's often said that fundraising is all about relationships, but nowhere is this truer than with major donors, where effective cultivation can mean the difference between regular but minor gifts and truly transformational support. Whether they be meetings, calls, invitations, tours, recognition events or anything else, make sure your cultivation efforts are having the biggest possible effect on donors and prospects.

Cultivation Helps Explore Next Moves

Going after major gifts often requires a much more sophisticated series of cultivation moves than is needed for lower-end gifts. And because you can't use the same friend-raising strategies with every prospect — they should be tailored to the interests and circumstances of each — it's important to select from many alternatives.

To help you plan individualized cultivation moves for each of your major gift prospects, develop a menu of cultivation categories, such as the example here, to guide your decision making. These categories can be used as a tool by individual development officers or in a group setting as a way to brainstorm what cultivation moves would be most appropriate with particular prospects.

Use of a cultivation possibilities menu also forces you to ask: "What's my most important objective with this prospect at this point in time?"

CULTIVATION POSSIBILITIES MENU

Prospect _____ Date _____

Objective	Steps To Be Taken
To involve one or more family members of the prospect....	1. _____ 2. _____
To recognize or honor the prospect....	1. _____ 2. _____
To help the prospect more fully understand and appreciate the work of our organization....	1. _____ 2. _____
To make the prospect more aware of the level of gift required....	1. _____ 2. _____
To better determine the prospect's potential funding interests....	1. _____ 2. _____
To engage the prospect in realizing greater ownership of our agency and its programs....	1. _____ 2. _____
Other objectives/steps....	1. _____ 2. _____

Craft a Cultivation Plan for Your Top 25

As you work at creating your yearly operational plan, anticipated major gift actions should be an integral part of that plan.

During your planning process, outline a plan of cultivation moves you intend to use for each of your organization's top prospects. Does that mean you will follow those cultivation moves to the letter? Not necessarily, but it will ensure that you have thought through how you intend to forge relationships with each probable donor, and the very act of identifying cultivation moves will give you a better idea of what needs to happen and when.

If you don't already have one, create a menu of cultivation moves, such as the example shown here, you can review as you consider appropriate actions for each of your top 25 or so prospects.

Including a schedule of anticipated cultivation moves in your yearly operational plan will ensure that everyone is getting deserved attention as they progress toward the realization of major gifts.

Menu of Cultivation Moves

- ❑ Meeting with a board member
- ❑ Invitation to join the board
- ❑ Personal call with focused objective
- ❑ Feature in magazine/newsletter
- ❑ Invitation to speak to students
- ❑ Invitation to participate in feasibility/planning study
- ❑ Invitation to host an event
- ❑ Facilities tour
- ❑ Meeting with president/CEO
- ❑ Bestow an honorary degree or some other award
- ❑ Invitation to join advisory board
- ❑ Meeting with faculty member/other employee
- ❑ Invitation to participate in strategic planning session

CULTIVATING MAJOR DONORS

Three-step Strategy for Securing First-time Discovery Visit

As a development officer for McKendree University (Lebanon, IL), Jeanine D. Simnick is expected to make numerous donor visits each month and reach out to new donor prospects on an ongoing basis.

To help manage her efforts, increase her efficiency, and document her progress in securing a first visit, Simnick has developed — through trial and error and ideas gleaned from "Developing Major Gifts" by Laura Fredricks — a three-step strategy that has resulted in increased success in securing first-time visits:

✓ **Step one: Letter of introduction.** Each donor prospect receives a letter of introduction that focuses on the importance of relationships, on and off campus. The letter states the purpose of Simnick's position and her desire to learn about the prospect's opinions and interests. At the end of the letter, she informs the donor that she will be calling within two weeks to introduce herself once more and to schedule a visit. When planning trips outside of the area, she mentions which week she will be traveling to the donor's location. After mailing the letter, she uses the Custom View Report feature in Raiser's Edge to print a call report sheet she can use to document notes taken during subsequent follow-up phone calls and visits.

✓ **Step two: Follow-up phone calls/e-mails.** Within two weeks of mailing the letters, she begins making phone calls. During the first call, she introduces herself, mentions the letter she mailed and suggests some possible dates to meet. If she gets the person's voice mail, she leaves her phone number but also lets the prospect know that she will call back. If she doesn't hear from the prospect, she calls him or her a second time, leaving the same message if she gets his or her voice mail.

"During the third attempt to call, if I still do not reach the person, I will leave my phone number once more, and state that if we are not able to connect at this time, he or she is always welcome to call me with an opinion or question," she says. "Calls are made several days to a week apart, depending on the timing of the letters and date of my trip to the prospect's area."

If she has an e-mail address for the prospect, she will e-mail instead of call on the third attempt. With each attempt, she says, she has found it worthwhile to call on different days of the week as well as to alternate the time of day the call is made, noting, "I have had great success reaching people on Friday afternoon."

If when making the calls, she discovers that the phone number is bad and can't find an alternate on switchboard.com or anywho.com, she sends a letter stating she had difficulty in reaching him or her (providing the phone number she used), and suggesting that he or she complete the enclosed response card. The letter closes with the statement, "Your continued interest in McKendree is very important to us."

✓ **Step three: Follow-up letter.** If there is no response after the third call or e-mail, she will send a follow-up letter stating that she has made several attempts to reach the person (providing the number she used), and that her intent is not to inundate the person with calls, but to simply offer an opportunity to ask questions and discuss McKendree's progress. "This letter has been successful in obtaining a response and discovering people were out of town when I made my calls," she says. At times, when making 20 to 30 calls a day, she has found that using Action Tracks in Raiser's Edge has improved her efficiency. "When I mark my first step complete, this function automatically generates the next step (call two) and sets a reminder," she says. "All actions are documented in Raiser's Edge as discovery steps."

Source: Jeanine D. Simnick, Development Officer, McKendree University, Lebanon, IL. Phone (618) 537-6823. E-mail: jdsimnick@mckendree.edu

---

Oct. 21, 2010

Address

Dear Mr. and Mrs....

McKendree University values its relationships with people — students, alumni, friends, parents, staff and faculty. These relationships exist on and off campus, across the country, and are the roots beneath McKendree's continued success.

As the Development Officer for Institutional Advancement, I would like to take a moment of your time to introduce myself. My name is Jeanine Simnick, and I have the great fortune of personally connecting with alumni and strengthening these important relationships. Not only do I focus on learning what the interests and opinions are of our alumni, I look for opportunities to engage individuals with the University's vision and future direction.

It would be my pleasure to share news of your alma mater, listen to your McKendree experiences and present you with a couple of alumni items. Within the next two weeks I will contact you to introduce myself once more and talk about an opportunity to chat with you personally. I am traveling to the Phoenix area the week of June 21 and hope you are available for a brief visit.

At any time you are welcome to contact me. I can best be reached at (618) 537-6823 or jdsimnick@mckendree.edu. I look forward to the opportunity to meet you, Mr. and Mrs. ...!

Warm regards,

Jeanine Simnick
Development Officer

CULTIVATING MAJOR DONORS

Engaging Gift Prospects Is First Step to Setting Visits

Q. What can we do to get prospects to accept visits from our fundraisers?

"Try asking them for advice on a specific issue that you know will interest them and bring them back to campus. For example, if your prospect is a former athlete, you could say, 'We're putting together an alumni advisory committee for the promotion of athletics and wanted your advice on how athletics shaped your college experience. We're looking for a few alumni to come back to campus and talk with current students....' If you go into the first meeting asking for advice, you'll get much better results. Make it clear that you are only asking for advice in the first meeting and work in giving after they are engaged. A cold first visit ask is not as successful as a two- to three-visit warm-up ask, even for annual fund gifts. Keep in mind that you're cultivating a lifelong relationship even though you're measured on fiscal year dollars."

— *Sean Devendorf, Director of Annual Giving and Alumni Relations, Friedman School of Nutrition, Tufts University (Boston, MA)*

"When seeking visits with alumni prospects, I have our development officers emphasize that they are seeking to personally connect with people to update them on the university and to explore associations and connections that can benefit a specific college, program or the university in general. I ask each development officer to be an 'honest broker.' That means that if someone they contact is not interested in their college, school or unit, but has a general interest in our university, that they bring that information back so that we can reassign the appropriate development officer to be in contact with that person. I also encourage our development officers to use other alums they work with and/or members of their advisory boards to be the primary contact with the prospect and to set up a meeting. People who say they do not want to meet with a development officer are added to a list and a development officer will recontact them a year or two later — if research has found they are good potential prospects — on the premise that their circumstances, mindset, etc. may have changed since we last contacted them."

— *Bruce Mack, Associate Vice President for Development and Alumni Relations, University of Nevada (Reno, NV)*

"I have successfully used two approaches to get visits with prospects — volunteers and focus groups. Use your volunteers (or closer alumni) to help open doors. Many of your alums may be skittish about meeting with you when the call comes from the advancement office, while they may be perfectly willing to meet with you and another alum if the call is from the volunteer. Assemble a focus group of alumni representative of those you are looking to visit and ask them how to approach this challenge and why this problem exists. This should provide some very meaningful direct approaches to addressing it."

— *Scott VanDeusen, Executive Director of Advancement Programs, St. John's University (Jamaica, NY)*

Know When to Hit the Brakes

You've met with a prospective donor several times to build a relationship and begin to explore funding opportunities. Each time you have felt positive about the progress being made. But this time was different. The prospect showed more hesitation about considering a major gift. What to do?

This is the when some development professionals get anxious, and instead of slowing down, hit the accelerator and push for a gift. That's the wrong approach.

If you meet with a *probable donor* — a term coined by philanthropic consultant Jerold Panas — who seems hesitant or reluctant, slow down. Give the person room to breathe. If the person feels pressure, the chance of a gift will quickly diminish.

Rather than push for a commitment, pinpoint the hesitancy. Ask a probing question. The issue may simply be a matter of timing, or perhaps the donor's funding interests are different than what you perceived them to be. Then leave on a positive note and agree to meet again.

Recognize that the final decision to make a major gift needs to come from within. After all, your goal should be to protect and nurture a long-term relationship that may result in multiple gifts and perhaps even a planned gift over time.

CULTIVATING MAJOR DONORS

Use Existing Endowments To Cultivate New Donors

One way to cultivate new endowment donors is to showcase your current endowment donors, says J. Richard Ely, Jr., owner, Strategic Fundraising Consultants (Providence, RI).

"Generate a list that shows all of your endowment funds, so that prospective donors can see that you have endowment funds that go back many years," Ely says. "Prospective donors can get a sense that you are keeping faith with donors."

For example, Ely says, showing that you are still honoring a 1922 donor's gift to purchase books for science tells donors you are good stewards of donors' gifts.

When you meet with donors, Ely says, show them this list and say, "Look at this list of distinguished people you are joining when you create an endowment fund."

Source: J. Richard Ely, Jr., Owner, Strategic Fundraising Consultants, Providence, RI. Phone (401) 274-3863. E-mail: rely@planned-giving.com

Address Donors' Privacy and Security Concerns

Some major donors place a priority on maintaining the privacy of their finances and giving habits. Others are more concerned about the security of sensitive information such as credit card numbers or address information. Either way, nonprofits have an obligation to do everything within their power to protect donors, says Heather Cleary, director of donor services at the Hispanic Scholarship Fund (HSF), San Francisco, CA.

"These are huge issues to many donors," Cleary says. "Whether they are giving online or sending in a check, they have concerns, and clearly articulated security and privacy policies definitely make some donors more likely to give. Sometimes it's just enough to give people that little push they need to get off the fence."

While virtually all nonprofits have such practices in place internally, Cleary says it is important to make them publicly available. Help crafting such a policy can be found in the form of the many free templates available on the Internet, she says.

Part of HSF's donor privacy policy is shown below. See the entire policy at: www.hsf.net/uploadedFiles/Support_HSF/Donor_Privacy%20_Policy_BillofRights.pdf

Source: Heather Cleary, Director of Donor Services, Hispanic Scholarship Fund, San Francisco, CA. Phone (877) 473-4636. E-mail: Hcleary@hsf.net. Website: www.hsf.net/Support HSF.aspx?id=2088

This excerpt of the donor privacy policy for the Hispanic Scholarship Fund (San Francisco, CA) details its donor bill of rights. Other sections of the four-page policy address privacy in data collection and use of data, data security and notification procedures.

Content not available in this edition

CULTIVATING MAJOR DONORS

Seven Ways to Make Donors Comfortable Enough to Give

To build major donors, you must first build trust between your organization and prospects. To strengthen that relationship:

1. **Have a donor bill of rights.** Post it where visitors can see it. Send a copy of it out, along with a thank-you note, to first-time donors.

2. **Follow up with first-time donors.** Make a call to that first-time donor to say thank you and find out why he/she chose you.

3. **Make sure the money goes where it's meant to go.** Ensure that restricted gifts go where they are supposed to and share the information with donors about that (e.g., If a donation is to fund summer camp programs, send photos out once camp is over).

4. **Be specific.** Go to donors with specific needs, not just asking for general donations.

5. **Meet face-to-face.** At least once a year, find a way to get in front of significant donors. Host a brunch with the CEO, have a VIP reception or offer to visit them at home.

6. **Make thank-you calls.** Donors like to hear from you, especially when you're not asking for money. Calling to say thanks or to ask their opinion on a new project or program shows that you feel their investment in your organization goes beyond their donations.

7. **Be thoughtful.** Consider why donors might make a gift to your organization. Also, think about what might keep them from making one.

Simple Thank-you Lunches Have Big Impact on Donors

Looking to secure sizable commitments from major donors? Consider taking them out to lunch — and not asking for money.

Ronald Sykes, headmaster emeritus and director of advancement at The Covenant School (Charlottesville, VA), took this approach in luncheon meetings with every major donor from the school's 25-year history — 36 donors in all.

"I didn't ask for a thing," Sykes says. "I thanked them for everything they've done, outlined developments planned for the school and asked them what had moved them to give to the school in the past."

The approach opened an organic and highly valuable dialogue, says Sykes, noting that most donors simply wanted news on the school's financial health and plans for particular programs, sports and facilities.

Sykes says he scrupulously avoided direct appeals, but financial support was nevertheless forthcoming. "Without any ask on my part, two parents made challenge pledges to increase parent participation in our annual fund — an issue that has been an ongoing challenge. One said he would give $25,000 if we could achieve more than 50 percent participation. Another offered to make an anonymous gift of $50,000 if we could get participation above 60 percent."

Source: Ronald Sykes, Director of Advancement, The Covenant School, Charlottesville, VA. Phone (434) 220-7327. E-mail: rsykes@covenantschool.org

Major Gift Essentials: Everything You Need to Know to Secure Big Gifts

SOLICITING TRANSFORMATIONAL GIFTS

At the end of the day, fundraising always comes down to making the ask. How you position your organization, how you present the funding opportunity, how you paint a picture of the future — all these considerations can mean the difference between a polite decline and the thoughtful silence that holds the potential for a long-term partnership. The following advice and suggestions will help you develop a solicitation that will get donors to "yes".

Make Compelling Case Statements Very Brief

Tom Ahern, principle of Ahern Communications, Ink (Foster, RI), shares a story about the importance of brevity in compelling case statements:

A college developed a 2,500-word statement for an upcoming campaign and started approaching top supporters with it. One prospect looked at the lengthy statement, scratched his head, and after several minutes of explanation asked if the campaign could be boiled down to the aim of furthering academic excellence. When the gift officer said it could, the man said, "Well, I support academic excellence. How much are you looking for today?"

The lesson to be learned? Charities often over-complicate the process.

"You need to be able to get the heart of your entire vision across in the first 30 to 50 words," Ahern says. "You need to be able to express your central aim in just a sentence or two. And if you can't do that, you probably don't really understand what you are doing and why."

Know What's Negotiable

As you strive to solidify a donor's gift commitment during the closing phase, remember what's negotiable. Then rely on what's negotiable to maximize the gift.

Here's a sample of negotiable items:

- ❑ The payout period of a pledge.
- ❑ The amount of the gift or pledge.
- ❑ Perceived perks.
- ❑ Adding to an outright gift with a planned gift.
- ❑ Naming opportunities.
- ❑ Certain funding restrictions.

How to Sell Your Vision to Donor Prospects

Behavioral research shows that donors are fundamentally skeptical about donating to nonprofits, says Tom Ahern, author and principle of Ahern Communications, Ink (Foster, RI). "The most ancient parts of our brain are concerned only with survival," Ahern says, "and they need a very compelling reason to part with hard-earned money."

A concise and compelling case statement is key to providing this reason, he says. Here, Ahern discusses some of the fine points of this important solicitation tool:

What is the bedrock of a successful case statement?

"Everything in a good case statement is focused on answering three key questions: Why this organization? Why now? Why should I care? You need to explain why your project is uniquely valuable and more worthy of investment than other projects. You need to explain why the donor should write a check today instead of next week or next year. And you need to explain why the donor should care about what your vision is and what you are trying to do."

How should a case statement be used? What is it designed to do?

"A case statement is a tool to be used in face-to-face solicitation. You don't send it to the prospect in advance; you bring it with you to the meeting. You have it in your hands to prompt the points you want to focus on, and you might open it up at times to illustrate a point or have the prospect look at something. When the meeting is over, the case statement can also be left with the prospect as he or she is considering a gift."

What does a good case statement look like? Pages of text? A short list of bulleted points?

"There is no formulaic answer, but in general you want to make the statement as short as possible. The core case for Yale's $3.2 billion Yale>>Tomorrow campaign was only 550 words. The rest of the document was pages and pages of photographs and provocative quotes about how uncertain the world can be and how important it is to plan for the future."

Development professionals have a great deal of information about their organization. What kinds of facts should be included in a case statement?

"There are two basic types of evidence: statistical and anecdotal. Research shows that donors respond far more strongly to one anecdote about one person than to any number of statistics. Stats should be used, but as a background that reinforces the central narrative. It's also important to know that research has shown people respond much more strongly to the story of a single child than the story of that child and a sibling. Adding even one other person to an anecdote makes it less effective, and adding more than that just crushes donor response."

What's the biggest misconception nonprofits have about making their case with prospects?

"Talking too much about themselves. People don't give *to* charities, they give *through* them. Unfortunately, charities often forget they are only a means for a donor to help solve a problem. I have seen case statements asking for $150 million in which the donor is never mentioned, the word you is never used. That is not an engaging practice and not a good way to get support."

Source: Tom Ahern, Principle, Ahern Communications, Ink, Foster, RI. Phone (401) 397-8104. E-mail: A2Bmail@aol.com

SOLICITING TRANSFORMATIONAL GIFTS

Five Rules for More Successful Fundraising

The difference between adequate fundraising and outstanding fundraising is often smaller than you think, says Jean Block, author and founding CEO of Jean Block Consulting (Albuquerque, NM). Drawing on decades of fundraising experience, Block shares five simple principles guaranteed to help nonprofits secure the resources they need and deserve.

1. **Remember the You:Me Ratio** — Fundraising is not about you and what you need; it's about the donor and what he needs in return for a gift. Review a solicitation letter for the number of YOUs (donor words) versus MEs (your agency words). Focus your writing and asking on the benefits to the donor, not the benefits to you.

2. **Ask for What You Want, or Take What You Get!** — Board volunteers are often not as successful as they could be, because they are afraid to ask for a specific amount. Instead, they say, "Can you help us?" or "Anything you can do would be greatly appreciated." Don't make a donor uncomfortable by making her name the amount. Ask for a specific amount and be ready to negotiate.

3. **Wait for the Person Who Can Say 'Yes'** — When contacting a potential funder, don't let the gatekeeper take your message or keep you from talking to the decision maker. Your energy, passion and enthusiasm can't be translated by someone else or captured on a while-you-were-out slip. If the potential funder isn't available, ask for voice mail and leave a message that you'll call back. Enthuse your message!

4. **Don't be Afraid of 'No'** — "'No' can be the beginning of a long and fruitful conversation," Block says. "If you are told 'no,' first say, 'Thank you! Thank you for taking my call and listening to my request.'" Then, ask the following three questions:

   ❑ What do I need to know to ask better next time?

   ❑ Now that you know who we are and what we offer, can you think of anyone else who might like to take advantage of this opportunity?

   ❑ If you can't give money at this time, is there any other way we might work together?

5. **Thank, Thank, Thank** — Spend as much time, energy and creativity on thanking as you did asking. Make it timely and meaningful. Connect the donor with the results of his/her gift. Focus on outcomes. "If you don't have time to thank donors," Block says, "you shouldn't even ask."

Source: Jean Block, President/CEO, Jean Block Consulting, Inc., Albuquerque, NM. Phone (505) 899-1520. E-mail: jean@jblockinc.com. Website: http://www.jblockinc.com

---

Be Alert to Timing Issues When Asking for Major Gifts

Although capability and inclination are two factors that weigh heavily in a potential donor's decision to make a major gift, appropriate timing of an ask is also crucial. Here are circumstances that can impact solicitation timing either positively or negatively:

- Sale or acquisition of a business.
- Marriage or divorce.
- Interest rates.
- Competition from other fundraising efforts.
- Death of a spouse or loved one.
- Sale or purchase of a residence.
- Issues related to children: birth, college tuition obligations, etc.
- Wide fluctuations in stock market overall or in one particular stock.
- General state of the economy.
- Career changes: promotions, demotions, bonuses, stock options.

Bring the Right Tone To Major Gift Solicitations

Confidence, urgency and optimism can all strike a chord with potential donors, but one shade of emotion stands out above all the rest, says Martin Leifeld, vice chancellor of university advancement at the University of Missouri-St. Louis (St. Louis, MO).

"I find having a certain gravitas in the room — like one is taking part in a very ennobling experience — is very effective," says Leifeld. "When donors reach a sober and considered conclusion in an atmosphere of seriousness, the experience can be amazingly powerful."

Source: Martin Leifeld, Vice Chancellor of University Advancement, University of Missouri-St. Louis, St. Louis, MO. Phone (314) 516-4278. E-mail: leifeldm@umsl.edu

SOLICITING TRANSFORMATIONAL GIFTS

Learn How to 'Listen the Gift'

Many fundraisers fail to work on two of the most important factors in securing major gifts — probing and listening — says fundraising consultant Jerold Panas of Jerold Panas, Linzy & Partners (Chicago, IL).

"If you do all the talking, you are in the spotlight (and) it is your agenda, not the donor's," he says. "As a result, you won't learn anything new about the prospective donor."

But if you listen 75 percent of the time and talk 25 percent of the time, Panas says, "you don't have to even ask for the gift. You will 'listen the gift.' By listening carefully, you will know precisely what will motivate the prospective donor and the amount you should ask for."

Listening is one skill that can be taught and learned, Panas says. He has developed an instrument called "Listen the Gift: A Guide to Effective Listening," that helps people measure their effectiveness in listening. The four-page, 58-question tool (shown in part, here) includes sections on concentration, relationship building and personal concerns.

For example, the instrument asks persons to gauge their listening quotient based on statements such as:

❑ Concentration: "When I talk with someone, I have a better recollection of what they said as opposed to what I said."

❑ Relationship building: "I attempt to gather more information about the other person by asking questions."

❑ Personal concerns: "I care greatly about people and those I meet and talk with, and they can sense that in my listening."

Persons rank their listening skills on a rating scale from 5 (always) to -2 (never). The total points tell the person their "listening quotient" from "Outstanding — You're great!" to "Active listening is an acquired talent — You should make an effort to improve your skills."

Panas uses this instrument in his workshops, asking attendees to review it and then using it to talk about how to improve listening skills. Individuals can also fill it out themselves and then ask a colleague, supervisor or spouse to fill it out for them and compare the results.

The guide is also a valuable staff exercise, says Panas, who says staff can take the test and then talk about the results to determine where they excel and where there may be room for them to improve listening skills and, ultimately, boost their ability to raise funds.

Content not available in this edition

Source: Jerold Panas, Jerold Panas, Linzy & Partners, Chicago, IL. Phone (312) 222-1212. E-mail: ideas@panaslinzy.com. Website: www.jeroldpanas.com

SOLICITING TRANSFORMATIONAL GIFTS

Get Donors to Say 'Yes' With These Simple Words

The right words can have a significant impact in conversations with current and potential donors, says Kevin Hogan (Eden Prairie, MN), author of the book, "The Psychology of Persuasion: How to Persuade Others to Your Way of Thinking."

In conversations, Hogan says, certain words can cause yes to happen.

Here, he explains why certain words prompt individuals to respond to a request with a "yes" instead of a "no":

Because

"Remember when you were a kid and your mother told you to clean your room?" says Hogan. "You said, 'Why?' and she said, 'Because I said so,' and you cleaned your room. You are literally programmed to do what a person asks after he says 'because.'" For example, "We would appreciate having your support because it will show the community how important this project is to the people we serve."

Imagine

"In order to create resistance-free communication, don't obligate the person to the task, simply ask them to imagine it," says Hogan. "No one objects because you aren't asking them to take an action, but rather, to watch a movie in their mind." For example: "Just imagine the Kevin Hogan Center for Cancer Research. Wouldn't that be wonderful?"

Now

"'Now' triggers a childhood-programmed piece of code to do what you're asked. Your mother told you to go to bed, you resisted, she said, 'Now,' and you went. 'Now' is a punctuation mark, but the more softly it comes across in a solicitation, the more likely the person will be to comply with the request." For example, "Our dream, which we hope you can fulfill, is that you make your gift now so we can count you among our pace-setting donors."

Don't

"(The word) 'don't' directs a person's behavior based on their inborn need to rebel against what they're not supposed to do," he says. "People don't like to have choices removed. When you tell a child, 'Don't touch the TV,' that's the thing they'll touch." For example, "Don't feel obligated to commit to the gift today."

Person's Name

"Nothing matters more to a person than his or her name," says Hogan. "Use it once, at the beginning. When you use a person's name once, the rapport value goes high, high, high. Use it a second time and it levels off. As you use it a third, fourth, fifth and sixth time, the rapport value goes way down. If you overuse it, people will feel as if they're being manipulated." For example: "Hi John, great to see you. I'm excited to tell you about the campaign."

Source: Kevin Hogan, International Consultant, Speaker, Corporate Trainer & Author, Eden Prairie, MN. Phone (612) 616-0732. E-mail: Kevin@kevinhogan.com. Website: www.kevinhogan.com

Turn a Donor's 'No' Into 'Yes'

After an otherwise smooth and successful solicitation meeting, your potential donor has just turned down your ask. What next?

Unfortunately, "most development officers don't ask questions after hearing that 'no,'" says Jerry Smith, founder of the development consulting firm, J.F. Smith Group (Auburn, AL).

Ask these five questions, Smith says, to turn that "no" into a "yes."

1. Say, **"Let me ask you a question. Are you saying, 'no,' because you have a problem with our nonprofit organization?"** Any major donor is already familiar with your organization and knows the work you do, so he or she will certainly confirm that there's no problem with the institution itself.

2. Then say, **"Let me ask you, is it this specific project?"** As most major gift requests are made to line up funding for a specific project, this will be your chance to learn if another project might interest your donor more.

3. Your third question should be, **"Is the amount I asked for a problem?"** As major donors have almost always donated before, you probably went into the meeting with a ballpark figure to ask. Most major donors are therefore comfortable with the amount of the ask — although if yours isn't, now is your opportunity to follow up with, "Your participation in this project is valuable to us. What can we do to have you be a part of this?"

4. **If the amount is still not what is causing the donor to say "no," ask a fourth question: "Is this a bad time?"** Smith says that, most likely, this will be the root of the problem. Your donor might say something like, "I've got two other pledges I have to pay off in the next 18 months." Follow up by asking a final question:

5. **"If I can show you how you can make a pledge that wouldn't start until 20 months out, would you consider that request?"** This ask should be for the same amount as your original ask — and there's a very good chance that with that last question, Smith says, you've just put your donor at ease and lined up a major gift!

Source: Jerry Smith, Founder, J.F. Smith Group, Auburn, AL, Phone (334) 502-5374. E-mail: JerrySmith@jfsg.com

SOLICITING TRANSFORMATIONAL GIFTS

Don't Try to Negotiate With Donors' Mandates

Major donors might be willing to negotiate many parameters of their giving, but geographic focus is not usually one of them, says Robert Evans, founder and managing director of the EHL Consulting Group of Willow Grove, PA.

"One donor might give nationally but prefer to keep money inside the country," Evans says. "Another might have an affinity for a particular region such as the Midwest or Pacific Northwest. A third might give generously, but only to local projects. These priorities are not usually open for discussion and challenging them is simply counterproductive in most cases."

Source: Robert Evans, Founder and Managing Director, The EHL Consulting Group, Inc., Willow Grove, PA. Phone (215) 830-0304. E-mail: Revans@Ehlconsulting.com

Prepare for Team Solicitation

If you're making calls in teams of two or three — one staff person and one or two volunteers — be sure the secondary solicitors are fully prepared.

As helpful as it can be to have a team rather than one person make the call, an unprepared team member can unintentionally dismantle what's been accomplished.

Avoid having a team member who:

- Fails to listen fully to the prospect.
- Has little or no background information about the prospect.
- Has yet to make a generous commitment to your organization.
- Talks too much.
- Lacks understanding about the project you wish to have funded.
- Isn't familiar with key facts or the history of your organization and its work.
- Has little or no previous involvement with your organization.

Get to 'Yes' Through Solicitation Scripting and Rehearsal

Have a sizable gift solicitation on the horizon? You might want to start practicing now, says Martin Leifeld, vice chancellor of university advancement at the University of Missouri–St. Louis (St. Louis, MO).

"Major gift solicitations can and should be well-scripted in advance," says Leifeld, who regularly rehearses his solicitations of prospective donors with staff members to the point of hammering out even the language he will use and the questions he will ask.

Scripting and rehearsal can improve many aspects of the solicitation process, says Leifeld. Among the areas he highlights are:

- ❑ **Relationships.** Finding people well-matched to a prospect's status, personality and interests is a vital part of the solicitation process, says Leifeld. Scripting a call in advance ensures that the right people will be in the room and that non-development participants are prepared for the role they will play.

- ❑ **Comfort level.** Development professionals get nervous no matter how many years are under their belt, says Leifeld. Prior rehearsal is what helps them move through any hesitation they might experience.

- ❑ **Tough questions.** Major solicitations often include questions that must be asked but which will create a certain amount of discomfort. Practicing these questions ahead of time and deciding which team member will ask them helps ensure they are not omitted, says Leifeld.

- ❑ **Varied responses.** "A donor will either agree to the gift, ask for time to consider, suggest a lower gift amount or decline," says Leifeld. Preparing strategies appropriate to each of these donor responses is key to effective solicitation.

- ❑ **Contingency plans.** The CEO of a major corporation once declined Leifeld's primary and back-up opportunities, and asked what else he had to offer. Luckily, says Leifeld, he and his team had talked through a number of projects before the meeting, and the CEO loved the third project they pitched.

To ensure development officers are adequately prepared, Leifeld asks them to fill out a short meeting summary form (shown below) before making solicitation calls. He says the worksheet provides a simple way to review fundraising basics like donor giving history, and gets staff thinking about meeting strategy and approach ahead of time.

Source: Martin Leifeld, Vice Chancellor of University Advancement, University of Missouri–St. Louis, St. Louis, MO. Phone (314) 516-4278. E-mail: leifeldm@umsl.edu

Content not available in this edition

Major Gift Essentials: Everything You Need to Know to Secure Big Gifts

MASTERING A RANGE OF PLANNED GIVING VEHICLES

In most organizations, planned giving is the source of most, if not all, major gifts. Planned gifts hold great financial potential, but their number and diversity can be daunting to even the most experienced fundraisers. The articles contained in this chapter will help you brush up on retained life estate agreements, charitable gift annuities, life insurance gifts and a number of other donor-friendly planned giving vehicles.

How to Develop a Planned Giving Marketing Plan

Before you launch your next marketing effort, make sure to include the four processes critical to the success of any marketing effort, says Ann McPherson, a marketing consultant with PG Calc (Cambridge, MA).

Specifically, McPherson says, your marketing effort plan should: 1) establish and articulate objectives; 2) define the strategy; 3) execute the tactics of the program within the budget; and 4) measure, report and refine.

"These four processes should be applied to both your annual plans and individual marketing initiatives," McPherson says. "They operate sequentially and are dependent on one another."

Here, McPherson further defines the four critical elements:

1. **Establish and articulate objectives.** Select both tangible, measurable goals that you can realistically achieve, and less quantifiable goals, she says: "Well-defined objectives allow marketers to articulate clearly and succinctly what the marketing program seeks to achieve; making the objectives measurable allows them to demonstrate success when it happens — or learn valuable lessons if the result is less successful than forecasted. Regardless of your specific objectives, one of the most important activities you'll need to engage in if your program is going to succeed is a consideration of organizational support, both external and internal. By establishing enthusiasm for your efforts, you'll ensure you have continued support to see it through to your projected outcomes."

2. **Define the strategy.** Conducting a SWOT analysis (Strengths, Weaknesses, Opportunities, Threats) of your organization's mission will help you draft a precise, carefully crafted value proposition, position your organization relative to its competitors and peers, and develop a deep understanding of the target audiences to use as leverage in the marketing process, she says: "Your target audiences may be varied and each segment requires different messaging, as well as different frequency of communications and information. Target audiences for most planned giving officers include long-term annual fund donors and major gift donors, as they have indicated a certain charity as being of particular interest to them; communities of advisors, as they have proven to be influential when it comes to their clients' charitable intent; and existing planned gift donors, who are often likely to make a repeat gift arrangement."

3. **Execute the tactics of the program within the budget.** If a program's objectives have been well-defined and the strategic planning diligently conducted, the executive phase should proceed smoothly, she says. One way to help you execute the tactics of the program within the budget is to build a spreadsheet listing the various activities that will help you accomplish your objectives and the dates associated with their development and implementation, says McPherson. "A spreadsheet can help you manage each task and provide all of your team members with a visual summary of their responsibilities. Typical data captured include 1) elapsed time for tasks, 2) the number of hours associated with each task, 3) the cost associated with each deliverable, and 4) ownership for each task. The process of building the spreadsheet is valuable in itself since it requires a marketer to spell out every step required in the execution of the program and indicates dependencies."

4. **Measure, Report, Refine.** Because of lengthy cultivation cycles, assigning dollars raised to any particular campaign may be impossible, she says "Recognize, instead, that each campaign you pursue produces some success even if it's hard to measure. This does not mean that you should stop measuring. Rather, it is better to keep paying attention to best practices; reviewing, documenting and improving upon internal benchmarks; and most importantly, talking to donors and prospects about their thoughts on communications they receive from your organization."

Source: Ann McPherson, Marketing Consultant, PG Calc, Cambridge, MA. Phone (888) 497-4970.
E-mail: amcpherson@pgcalc.com. Website: www.pgcalc.com

MASTERING A RANGE OF PLANNED GIVING VEHICLES

Five Tips for Making Planned Giving Work for You

Officials at Lawrence University (Appleton, WI) have spent the last two years revamping planned giving efforts. Through that process, Associate Vice President of Major and Planned Giving Barbara Stack says she has one rule of thumb when it comes to creating and improving planned giving programs: "Keep it simple. Ninety percent of planned gifts are made through bequests, so focus energy on promoting them."

In promoting bequests, Stack says, keep this top-of-mind: "The most compelling messages for bequest promotion ... focus on legacy, dreams and ensuring that the donor's values live on through the organizations they care about."

Stack identifies five specific guidelines that Lawrence University officials are using to make their planned giving programs stronger:

1. **Talk to younger donors about retirement assets.** Stack says this allows them to consider your organization earlier in life, which means they are less likely to need convincing later.

2. **Remember that getting started in planned giving doesn't need to be expensive.** "There is so much information, good material, solid advice and quality vendors in our line of work," she says. "Don't get caught up in the fancy tools unless you have trusted advisors who will work with you to do it right (e.g., CGAs, trusts, real estate, etc.)."

3. **Put your donors and your mission front and center.** "This is the best and most effective way to raise funds generally, but especially with planned gifts," says Stack. "Allow your best marketing partners — those who have already 'done it' — to feel great about their decision by allowing them to share their philanthropic journey. Allow the beneficiaries of your mission to express their own thanks to help illustrate what gifts accomplish."

4. **Have a quality Web presence** and piggyback your planned giving message with other communications from your organization.

5. **Measure your planned giving efforts by tracking meaningful contacts and visits with prospects and donors.** Provide stellar follow up and stewardship, and ensure you have the knowledge and resources to respond to inquiries.

"Most importantly, do not lose sight of why you are doing what you are doing," says Stack. "Planned gifts are not great because of tax advantages or glossy brochures or newsletters. They are another means to an end of fulfilling a donor's wishes to help your organization because it matters to them. If you always focus on the mission and helping donors find ways to support that mission . . . you will be doing your best work for your cause and your donors."

Source: Barbara J. Stack, Associate Vice President of Major and Planned Giving, Lawrence University, Appleton, WI. Phone (920) 832-6546. E-mail: barbara.j.stack@lawrence.edu

Planned Giving Requires Donor-centric Focus

Barbara Stack, associate vice president of major and planned giving at Lawrence University (Appleton, WI), discusses some of the challenges university officials have encountered and changes they have made through a recent two-year renovation of the university's planned giving efforts:

What sort of unique things are you working on in the area of planned giving?

"We developed a unique peer-outreach approach to our program, giving it a distinct Lawrence 'face.' We have about 35 volunteers who are members of our legacy recognition society who assist us in promoting planned giving to their fellow alumni and constituents who live in their regions across the country. The members help us raise visibility and recruit new members by hosting small parties with prospects, writing notes thanking new members, providing testimonials at events and in printed and electronic materials, serving in leadership roles for planned gift promotion as they approach milestone reunions and advising us on our website and printed marketing materials."

What have been your biggest challenges in terms of planned giving and how have you worked to overcome them?

"Our challenges stem from those things we cannot control, like fiscal caution resulting from the recent economic climate. This has provided us with both challenge and opportunity. Over the past couple of years, our donors and prospects have generally been skittish about making any changes to their financial or long-term plans, because they are uncertain about the future. We've addressed those concerns by being patient, continuing to focus on our mission and assuring donors that we work on their timeline and will be here when they're ready. At the same time, our donors have been more receptive to discussing how they might accomplish their philanthropic vision and dreams without jeopardizing their current situation. Due to these conversations, we were able to help our planned gift donors and prospects feel satisfaction by participating in our capital campaign through joining our legacy society and estimating future gifts that could be counted in our campaign."

MASTERING A RANGE OF PLANNED GIVING VEHICLES

Ask Donors to Complete an Intention Form

At the Fred Hutchinson Cancer Research Center (Seattle, WA), an intention form allows planned giving donors to clearly communicate various aspects of their plans in writing, says Lynette A. Klein, senior director of planned giving.

The form gathers contact information, gift details, recognition options and options for memorial recognition, as well as the specific amount or percentage of the planned gift (and estimated amount, if applicable).

"A lot of donors include a percentage of what they are donating to a charity or charities in their will," Klein says, "and the value of that percentage can change a lot from the time they fill it out until the gift is made, so many do not include the estimated amount."

The form is available online and in print form, Klein says, noting that while few people currently fill it out online, center officials hope to increase that number as online giving of planned gifts increases.

The print form, shown here, is a four-panel document used by the center's frontline fundraisers and given to anyone seeking information about planned gifts.

"The form is useful in a couple of ways," she says. "It tells donors about the type of information that is helpful for us to know even if they don't fill it out. Others fill it out, which provides us with information that allows us to have a written confirmation of how a donor wishes their gift to be recognized during their lifetime."

The form's primary value to the center, says Klein, is that it allows them to talk to the donor about their recognition options and their wishes for how the gift is used, "I like the form because it lists different recognition options that we can look at with the donor and discuss with them."

Source: Lynette A. Klein, Senior Director of Planned Giving, Fred Hutchinson Cancer Research Center, Seattle, WA. Phone (206) 667-2754.
E-mail: lklein@fhcrc.org

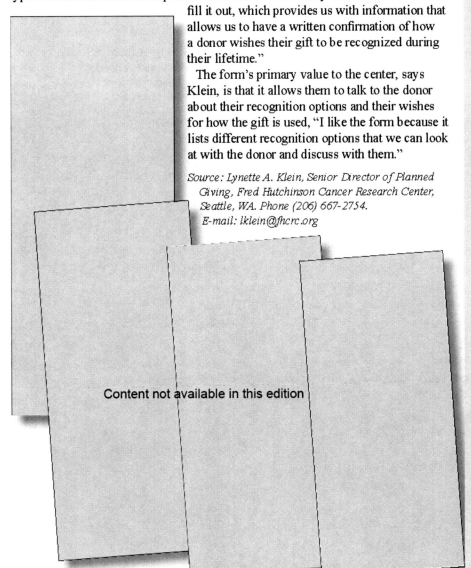

Content not available in this edition

Three Practical Strategies For Promoting Bequests

Since bequests are the most popular form of planned giving, it makes sense to continually promote them to your constituency. Here are three varied strategies for keeping the topic of bequests before your public:

1. **During any type of public gathering, never miss an opportunity to invite those present to consider your charity in their estate plans.** Whether your invitation is subtle or direct, mentioning the topic says it's important to your organization's future. If appropriate, state, "If you have made provisions but not informed us, please do."

2. **Don't be shy about publicizing the realization of a bequest.** The more examples the public sees, the more they realize your organization must be worthy of such gifts. These examples also provide you with additional opportunities to broadcast key messages: "Our board of trustees has approved a policy whereby all undesignated bequests will be directed to our endowment, thus perpetuating the donor's generosity for generations to come."

3. **Identify persons who share their intentions to include your charity in their estate plans and are willing to assist in encouraging others to do the same.** Determine ways such persons can help you promote bequests — testimonials at public functions, profiles in your newsletter or magazine, accompanying you on planned gift visits — and make use of their example. Engaging such willing individuals in your planned gift program will make them feel even more committed to your cause.

MASTERING A RANGE OF PLANNED GIVING VEHICLES

Advisory Council Focuses on Boosting Planned Gifts, Educating Community

A planned gift advisory council is having a major impact on planned giving at Wentworth-Douglass Hospital & Health Foundation (Dover, NH).

According to Deborah Shelton, vice president of philanthropy & chief philanthropy officer, the foundation is slated to receive at least 50 new planned gifts, with approximately 100 donors participating in its planned giving program.

Shelton credits much of that activity to the advisory council that includes estate-planning attorneys, financial planners, benefit professionals, certified public accountants, trust officers and other allied professionals.

The council meets five times a year. Meetings begin with a half-hour open forum about the hospital, followed by a business meeting. Members are expected to assist in identifying and nurturing persons capable of making a planned gift to the foundation, support the foundation themselves through gifts to the annual appeal and attend planned meetings and workshops as their schedules permit.

The members also offer a community education series, educating the public on issues involved with planned giving (see box, left).

To further engage these valued professionals and make them feel invested in the hospital and health foundation, Shelton says, she and her staff invite them to all open houses and special events.

Source: Deborah Shelton, Vice President of Philanthropy & Chief Philanthropy Officer, Wentworth-Douglass Hospital & Health Foundation, Dover, NH. Phone (603) 740-2894. E-mail: Deborah.Shelton@wdhospital.com

Community Education Series Educates Public on Planned Giving

A major role the planned gift advisory council at Wentworth-Douglass Hospital & Health Foundation (Dover, NH) fulfills is educating the community about issues related to planned giving. One way the council accomplishes this is through its community education series.

Series offerings for 2011 focus on a variety of topics while engaging experts with a wide range of professional expertise, including:

- **"Charitable Planning: Doing Well by Doing Good"** with Bernie Lebs and Patrick F. Olearcek, JD, CLU, ChFC, MassMutual Financial Group

- **"The Economy and Markets — Score-card of 2010 Predictions and Top 10 Predictions for 2011"** with Jay Levy, Merrill Lynch & Jared Watson, BlackRock Private Investors

- **"How to 'Do' Estate Planning With or Without the Federal Estate Tax"** with Bruce Johnson, Johnson & Associates & Tom Levasseur, The Beacon Retirement Group

- **"How to Do More With What You Have: Leveraging your Legacy"** with Robert Boulanger, Oppenheimer & Co., Inc. & Ken Money, Money Law Offices

- **"Veteran's Benefit"** with Rich Hilow, Financial Advisor, Edward Jones

- **"College Financial Planning"** with Melanie Dupuis, CPA, CCPS, Larry Raiche & Company CPAs

- **"Get the Facts"** A Reverse Mortgage Educational Event with Tom Torr, Cochecho Elder Law Associates & Kathleen Burke, Wells Fargo Home Mortgage

- **"Guardianship and Powers of Attorney — When Kids Become the Parents"** with Stephanie Burnham, Stephanie K. Burnham & Associates

- **"Re-Thinking Retirement Planning"** with Tom Levasseur, The Beacon Retirement Group & Karen Zaramba, Hunter Advisor Group, A Capital L member firm

- **"Saving Employee Benefit Costs While Keeping Employees Happy"** with Mark Jacobsohn, RELAYER Benefits Group, LLC

- **"Changes in Taxation Due to Current Political Environment that Impact Retirement, Investment and Planned Giving"** with Dave Verno, CPA, Leone, McDonnell & Roberts, PA

Content not available in this edition

MASTERING A RANGE OF PLANNED GIVING VEHICLES

Are You Ready for CGAs?

Charitable gift annuities (CGAs) — binding financial agreements between a nonprofit and a major donor — can be a great way to acquire large-scale donations. Yet, only a small percentage of nonprofits in the United States offer CGAs to major donors because of the planning and paperwork involved.

How do you know if your nonprofit is prepared to take on the added risk, responsibility — and reward — CGAs bring?

S.C. Chase Adams, managing director of Adams Associates (Ft. Lauderdale, FL), a law firm specializing in fundraising and estate preservation strategies, suggests referencing your organization's strengths and weaknesses against this five-point checklist:

1. **Are your books impeccable?** In a CGA with a donor, your organization is legally responsible for investing the donor's money in such a way as to guarantee payments to the donor, possibly for decades, requiring extra — and precise — accounting.

2. **How solid is your organization's long-term outlook?** With CGAs, nonprofits receive full ownership of the gift upon the donor's death. This is, of course, not something you can plan for, so the rest of your organization's long-term prospects need to be strong in the interim.

3. **What staff resources can you allocate or increase for the sake of CGAs?** The time, energy and expense of administering a CGA program can be onerous and expensive, says Adams. Tasks include record-keeping for each CGA account and a lengthy registration process each state requires before a nonprofit can enter into CGAs.

4. **What assets do you already have?** In some states, a nonprofit must pledge a percentage of assets as collateral to insure the donor's payments. Other states require that a nonprofit pledge all of its assets to qualify for CGA status.

5. **How much can you afford to financially invest in administering CGAs?** Although the adage usually applies to the for-profit sector, spending money to make money definitely applies to any nonprofit organization seeking CGAs.

Source: S.C. Chase Adams, Managing Director, Adams Associates, Fort Lauderdale, FL. Phone (954) 449-4970. E-mail: info@chaseadams.net. Website: www.financialarchitect.com

Turn Current Donors Into Estate Donors and Vice Versa

Frank Robertson, director of planned giving at the University of Minnesota Foundation (Minneapolis, MN), says that when it comes to fundraising, "we don't look at individuals as being either only estate donors or only current donors. Ideally, we think they should be both, and we think that, given the right circumstances, many will be."

Accordingly, Robertson and his staff encourage multiple forms of giving. One technique they use is what is known as the double ask. "The idea is that whenever you are asking for a major gift or an annual gift, you also bring up the idea of including the university in your estate plans," he says. "It's a relatively low-pressure approach and many of our development officers have come to really believe in it."

A robust stewardship process is another key to multiplying support, he says. All donors of future gifts, regardless of whether the amount is disclosed, receive membership in the university's Heritage Society. This introduces them to the stewardship process, which is important, according to Robertson.

"If someone is planning on establishing a scholarship upon their death, might they not want to start realizing that good work during their lifetime?" he says. "We find that including estate donors in the stewardship process not only cements their relationship with us, but often leads to other outright gifts."

Source: Frank Robertson, Director of Planned Giving, University of Minnesota Foundation, McNamara Alumni Center, Minneapolis, MN. Phone (612) 625-0893. E-mail: Rober038@umn.edu

MASTERING A RANGE OF PLANNED GIVING VEHICLES

Don't Overlook the Profitable Possibilities of Retained Life Estate Gifts

Content not available in this edition

Every real estate gift is uniquely challenging, says Phillip Purcell, vice president of planned giving and endowment stewardship, Ball State University Foundation (Muncie, IN.)

Purcell answers questions and shares insights on a class of donations known as retained life estate (RLE) gifts, which the planned giving expert says is a gift option nonprofit organizations often overlook:

What is a retained life estate gift?

"It's an irrevocable gift of the remainder interest in a donor's personal residence or farm. The donor keeps a life estate, retains the right to live on and use it during his or her lifetime, and upon death it passes to the charitable institution (see illustration)."

How does that differ from bequeathing a home in a will?

Retained Life Estate

DONOR

Transfer future interest in property via deed

1

2

CHARITABLE ORGANIZATION

• Receives income tax deduction
• Remains in home for life

"Revocability is one of the big differences. Bequests are revocable, and some people like the flexibility this offers. They like having more control over the home or farm, and being able to sell it should they need the cash. RLE gifts are irrevocable and less flexible in some ways, but offer many advantages as well."

What are some of these advantages?

"Primarily tax benefits. Because the gift is irrevocable, the donor can take an income tax charitable deduction (based on their age and the value of the property) in the year the gift is made, rather than waiting until the end of life. The transfer is not subject to capital gains tax, and the property passes free of federal estate tax as long as the life estate is left to a charitable institution.

"From the charity's perspective, a major benefit is the absence of probate. Because RLE is irrevocable, it is not subject to probate and therefore escapes the fees and delays associated with that process."

When do gifts of RLE make the most sense?

"There are two primary scenarios. The first is when the charity wants to use the land itself, for expanding a campus or building a camp for kids or something like that. The second involves land, which the charity doesn't want to use, but which is valuable and likely to become more valuable over time — real estate like farmland, property in the path of development or land in resort or vacation areas.

"In either situation, a gift of RLE allows the donor to retain use of the property while still ensuring it ends iup n the hands of the charity."

Source: Philip Purcell, Vice President for Planned Giving and Endowment Stewardship, Ball State University Foundation, Muncie, IN. Phone (765) 285-8312. E-mail: ppurcell@bsu.edu

MASTERING A RANGE OF PLANNED GIVING VEHICLES

What Should An Endowment Agreement Address?

Portland State University Foundation (Portland, OR) requires an endowment agreement form to request establishment of a new endowed account for lecture-ships, chairs, professorships, scholar-ships, or in support of a department or program.

Becky Hein, chief financial officer, answers questions about the endowment agreement, shown at right:

Why is it important to have an endowment agreement?

"Since an endowment fund is of permanent duration, the endowment agreement allows us to document the donor's intent for long-term use of the funds. We have policies related to investment management, spending distributions and management fees, and the endowment agreement confirms that the donor agrees with these policies. It also allows the university to accept and agree to the terms proposed by the donor."

What key elements should an endowment agreement address?

"An endowment agreement should address the following:

☐ That the fund is intended to be an endowment (of permanent duration).

☐ Any restrictions on use of the funds.

☐ That the nonprofit may determine policies for investment of the funds, expenditure appropriations (commonly called spending distributions) and the assessment of management fees (In other words, the agreement shouldn't dictate how the funds are invested or managed, but should leave that to the policies of the nonprofit's board of directors.)

☐ Flexibility in the restriction of the funds due to changing circumstances as long as the nonprofit attempts to reasonably follow the original donor intent. (This is useful if the curriculum changes, grading systems change, etc., and the purpose of the fund is no longer relevant.)

☐ The nonprofit's responsibilities so

Content not available in this edition

that the donor is assured the funds will be handled responsibly and prudently.

"The signature lines should confirm that this agreement represents the intent of the donor and that the nonprofit accepts these terms and believes they will be of benefit to the institution (e.g., the non-profit agrees to fund the professor-ship or lectureship)."

In what ways should an endowment agreement be different from any other major gift agreement?

"It should be different because its nature is long-term and it addresses long-term issues such as investment management, on-going fees and changing environ-

ments that may alter the usefulness of the purpose of the fund."

How is the endowment agreement used after it is signed and dated?

"The department or program that benefits from the funds receives a copy for their files. The foundation receives a copy for their files. Both areas are responsible for compliance with the terms of the agreement. The donor also receives a copy to document the agreement."

Source: Becky Hein, Chief Financial Officer, Portland State University Foundation, Portland, OR. Phone (503) 725-5881. E-mail: heinbe@pdx.edu

MASTERING A RANGE OF PLANNED GIVING VEHICLES

Soliciting Life Insurance Gifts

Accepting gifts of life insurance policies can be lucrative, but it can also be problematic, depending on how the gift is made, says Adam Aptowitzer, a lawyer with Drache Aptowitzer (Ottawa, Ontario, Canada).

"If the individual names the charity as beneficiary, that is easy and the nonprofit typically doesn't know about the gift until the donor's death," Aptowitzer says. But if the person donates a policy while he/she is living, the nonprofit must deal with the premium, he says. "If the nonprofit can't pay the premium, the donation might be worthless, although the nonprofit could secure a donation of the premium until the donor dies."

A major advantage of life insurance policies as gifts, he says, is that they can have a large payout for a small investment.

One disadvantage, says Aptowitzer, is the potential risk to a nonprofit's reputation related to accepting such gifts from donors who may later realize they still need the policy (and may be uninsurable by then), or there are dependents left with no means of support other than those donated policies.

Paula Straub, president, Save Gains Tax LLC (San Marcos, CA), a former investment advisor representative and current insurance agent, agrees that in the right circumstances, gifts of life insurance policies can be advantageous for nonprofits. However, she says, in today's cash-strapped nonprofit environment, large monthly premiums can strain a nonprofit's resources.

Alternatives to turning away a gift based on inability to pay the premium are to ask the donor to sell the policy to a life settlement company and donate cash proceeds to the nonprofit, or for the nonprofit to accept the gift and sell it to a life settlement company itself, says Straub.

Here is a sampling of life settlement companies:

- The Life Settlement Company of America (www.lscoa.com)
- IMS Associates (www.imssettlements.com)
- Legacy Benefits (www.legacybenefits.com)
- Integrity Capital Partners (www.integrityp.com)
- Life Policy Group (www.lifepolicygroup.com)

Sources: Adam Aptowitzer, Lawyer, Drache Aptowitzer, Ottawa, Ontario, Canada. Phone (613) 237-3300. E-mail: adamapt@drache.ca
Paula Straub, President, Save Gains Tax LLC, San Marcos, CA. Phone (760) 917-0858. E-mail: savegainstax@gmail.com

Procure a Large Financial Injection With Immediate Funding

A 2007 IRS ruling allows individual donors to provide a large sum of cash to a nonprofit — given immediately, through a single transaction, at no cost to either the nonprofit or donor.

"The impact of this is often equal to several fundraisers and allows an individual donor to make an immediate and meaningful contribution to his or her charity," says S.C. Chase Adams (Ft. Lauderdale, FL), attorney and planned giving consultant who serves as general counsel for the Planned Giving Foundation and Good Steward Ministries.

Adams describes this financial vehicle as "immediate funding."

Through immediate funding, a donor can deposit IRA or non-IRA funds into a private account that is held, for a predetermined period, by a designated charity. The charity immediately receives a portion of the original deposit, while at the end of the designated time period, the entire original sum is returned to the donor or his/her estate.

A simple analogy to explain immediate funding is to think of a person opening a CD account at a bank. Say the person deposits $1 million into a long-term CD, understanding that the bank will pay a $30,000 return at the term's end. The bank also intends to make money by reinvesting the deposit. While the depositor will see $30,000 in interest at the term's end, in total the bank may raise up to $80,000 off the initial deposit. The bank creates $50,000 in income with the depositor's money at no cost to the depositor.

Now replace the word "charity" for "bank" in the above scenario for a basic understanding of immediate funding.

Adams, who has handled estate planning for 25 years, finds immediate funding works best with high-net-worth individuals who have at least $750,000 in an IRA or investable assets of at least $1 million. More importantly, Adams says, the individual should be an existing annual donor who contributes at least $15,000 a year, as this is the sort of dedicated donor who would be most interested in using immediate funding.

Immediate funding solves a very pressing problem for nonprofits, says Adams, "It allows a wealthy donor to be generous to a charity without having to feel that he is taking that money away from his grandkids," which is a concern that often precludes charities from receiving large donations.

Adams' first step in arranging an immediate funding transaction is to talk to the charity's attorney or the individual donor's attorney. Why? "Quite honestly, unless you're an attorney, you will not believe that immediate funding is possible," he says. "However, every attorney will recognize it as valid and then be able to reassure the client or the charity that, in fact, it is perfectly legal."

Source: S.C. Chase Adams, CEO, Adams Associates, Ft. Lauderdale, FL. Phone (954) 449-4970. E-mail: info@FinancialArchitect.com

Major Gift Essentials: Everything You Need to Know to Secure Big Gifts

CAPITAL CAMPAIGNS AND NAMING OPPORTUNITIES

Capital campaigns harness the power of peer reinforcement and collective giving. Naming opportunities tap into donors' fundamental desire for legacy and recognition. Taken together, the two represent an enormous source of potential revenue and an area of fundraising with which no development officer should be unfamiliar.

How to Begin a Planning Study for a Major Capital Campaign

When considering a major capital campaign, many nonprofits turn to outside counsel to perform a campaign feasibility or planning study. A consultant interviews the people/businesses most likely to support a capital campaign and makes a recommendation about how much they believe your organization could potentially raise.

How do you choose the best consultant for this important task?

The first step is knowing when your organization is ready to take that first step and hire a consultant, says John M. Bouza, president and founder of the fundraising consultant firm, CanFund, The Canadian Centre for Fundraising (Ottawa, Ontario, Canada).

"Consultants are experts in their fields ... blessed with imagination," says Bouza. "As outsiders to your organization, consultants can judge its strengths and weaknesses with objectivity, see beyond the day-to-day routine and can help you position your organization for long-term growth."

Bouza says nonprofits may consider hiring a consultant under these circumstances:

✓ When you are embarking on a new method of fundraising, such as direct mail, a capital campaign or a planned giving program — especially if your organization has outgrown past fundraising activities and needs to transform itself into a larger, stable and professionally managed organization.

✓ When outside circumstances or opportunities suddenly call for more efficient and effectual fundraising, such as the planning of a new facility, the sudden need for increased visibility, or the potential for a campaign-starting endowment.

✓ When hiring or reinvigorating fundraising staff, you may need a consultant to supervise the selection process or to oversee training sessions.

Once your organization has decided to hire a consultant, Bouza says to create a request for proposal (RFP) to let prospects understand your organization and its needs fully before engaging in business together. For details on doing so, see the box, right.

Source: John M. Bouza, John Bouza, President and Founder, CanFund, The Canadian Centre for Fundraising, Ottawa, Ontario, Canada. Phone (613) 299-6699. E-mail: jbouza@canfund.org. Website: canfund.org

Content not available in this edition

CAPITAL CAMPAIGNS AND NAMING OPPORTUNITIES

Anatomy of a Lucrative Capital Campaign

In October 2008, officials with Connecticut College (New London, CT) publicly launched a $200 million comprehensive campaign that will run through 2013. The campaign calls to raise $100 million for campaign endowment (supporting professorships, study-away programs, financial aid, and interdisciplinary academic centers), $50 million for capital projects and facilities and $50 million for annual giving/annual fund.

Claire Gadrow, assistant vice president for advancement, shares key elements that are combining to build campaign success:

Timing — The campaign reached the $100 million mark in June 2009, but was not announced until autumn, during a combined trustee weekend/welcome-back event.

Message — Efforts focus on the school's history, what the school has achieved with funds throughout history, and who helped it to happen.

Staff — The advancement department of 40 staff, divided into alumni relations, annual funds, major gifts, planned giving, advancement services, research, stewardship, corporate foundation and government relations. The major gifts team includes a director, three officers, director of leadership giving, assistant vice president, vice president and college president. Each major gift officer has a portfolio of about 300 prospects.

Structure — All gifts (major gifts, annual gifts, planned gifts, reunion giving) count toward the campaign. All gifts to annual fund go directly into the college's operating budget. All bequests for less than $250,000 go to the annual fund; above $250,000 go towards campaign endowment, allowing the annual fund to be more nimble.

Strategies —

✓ Set benchmark goals — short-term, high-profile fundraising priorities for specific projects. The recent goal of $8 million for a fitness facility was met by six donors; another, $5 million for dorm renovation, was paid for by 10 donors.

✓ Consider every ask a triple ask — an annual fund ask, bequest discussion and campaign gift ask. A $25,000 annual fund donor may not be ready to talk about a $500,000 major gift, but if you focus on the immediate need for income, the donor will be receptive. If the donor can't give directly, ask for a step gift or charitable gift annuity, and 18 months later, have the outright gift conversation.

✓ Don't put off talking about planned giving. Planned giving currently makes up 25 percent of the Connecticut College campaign.

✓ Publicly make it about the bottom line.

✓ Make phone appeals and e-mail appeals rather than press appeals, and explain to prospects how you are saving money.

✓ Have donors sponsor necessary events, and advertise your financial diligence therein, it builds community. At the beginning of the economic slump, alumni attendance at Connecticut College was up 50 percent.

✓ Don't scale back travel — it is too important to maintain those relationships.

Source: Claire Gadrow, Assistant Vice President for Advancement, Connecticut College, New London, CT. Phone (860) 439-2439. E-mail: Claire.gadrow@conncoll.edu. Website: www.conncoll.edu/giving/

Decide On Donor Recognition Prior to Capital Campaign

When someone makes a significant gift, how do you recognize and celebrate that donor's generosity?

One option worth considering is purchasing naming plaques for buildings, rooms, equipment or other items purchased with donors' major gifts.

Ideally, determine exact methods of donor recognition during the planning phase of your capital campaign, as doing so allows you to best budget for such well-deserved recognition. And if you are mid-campaign, take time to regroup and set recognition standards, taking into account gifts received to date.

To create appropriate recognition for your campaign, answer these questions:

1. What form of recognition will be given to each publicized naming gift opportunity — plaques with individual donors' names? A plaque that lists all major donors?
2. Will the various forms of recognition have any degree of consistency?
3. How much are you prepared to spend for donor recognition?
4. Will the type of recognition given be appropriate for the gift size?
5. Where will each plaque be physically placed?
6. In addition to permanent recognition at your facility, will the donor receive some token of appreciation to display at home or work?
7. Will you coordinate a celebration, open house or other event to publicly thank all donors at the campaign's conclusion? How much are you willing to spend for that?
8. Is there a minimum gift amount for which donors will receive special recognition?
9. What process will be followed to ensure donors select the name or names they want included along with proper spelling?

Answers to these and other questions will help ensure donors are appropriately recognized and associated recognition costs are covered.

CAPITAL CAMPAIGNS AND NAMING OPPORTUNITIES

Consistency Is Key in Leveraging Naming Opportunities

While naming opportunities are among the most dependable sources of revenue for advanced institutions, the sale of naming rights — equal parts art and science — is not as simple or straightforward as it may seem. Bobby Couch, executive director of major gifts, Clemson University Athletics (Clemson, SC), shares valuable insights on this fundraising method:

Philosophically, how should organizations approach the sale of naming rights?

"Many organizations are too quid pro quo, and the sale of naming rights becomes almost like selling a piece of real estate. At Clemson, we try to make naming opportunities more a part of donor stewardship, more of a way for donors to feel close and connected to the institution they are supporting."

On what should a naming rights policy focus?

"Consistency and equivalency. You want to make sure that X amount of donation receives X amount of recognition, regardless of the donor or the program donated to. So our policy (lower box, right) clearly defines the size of plaque, size of lettering, the font used to recognize different levels of gift. That way everything is consistent."

How should an organization go about pricing naming opportunities?

"There are four steps you need to go through:
1. First, you need to go through your facilities and collect all your inventory — all the rooms, offices, lockers, fields, etc.
2. Next, you need to categorize the inventory — what is high visibility or low, what is in public traffic ways, what will be named in perpetuity and what might be moved or repurposed in the future.
3. When you begin pricing things, you need to research what your peer institutions are charging for similar assets.
4. Last, you need to ensure that your prices are consistent with each other, that comparable opportunities have comparable prices."

Does consistency mean premium naming opportunities should be avoided?

"No. Donors understand that you will take the prestige of a program into consideration when pricing its facilities. If your men's tennis team regularly wins major tournaments or your fine arts program is ranked in the top 10 nationwide, the right to name those elements will naturally command a higher price."

Are expiration clauses on naming opportunities appropriate?

"There is somewhat of an industry trend in that direction, particularly with corporate donors. With the frequency of mergers and acquisitions, corporate names that make sense today can be obsolete in a few years. For that reason, we tend to limit our corporate naming to five- and 10-year terms."

How does the sale of naming rights differ for facilities under construction?

"There are two rules of thumb with new construction. The first is that naming rights for the entire facility should be priced at 25 percent of construction costs or more. The price to name the new $10 million swimming center, for example, should not be less than $2.5 million. Secondly, you want all your other naming rights to generate more revenue than construction costs, ideally up to around 150 percent. So you would want all the rest of the naming opportunities for the center to produce around $12.5 million."

What about morality clauses or guidelines?

"The advancement staff at Clemson have pretty wide latitude for any gifts under $1 million. For anything over that, there is a named gifts committee that goes through a very thorough due diligence and considers any issues that might reflect poorly on the institution. The committee can also revisit the naming if an incident occurs with the donor at a later date."

Source: Bobby Couch, Executive Director of Major Gifts, Clemson University Athletics/IPTAY, Clemson, SC. Phone (864) 656-0361. E-mail: Jcouch@clemson.edu

---

Lean Toward Higher End When Setting Naming Price

Bobby Couch, executive director of major gifts, Clemson University Athletics (Clemson, SC), shares his thoughts on the biggest mistake in selling naming rights, and how to avoid it:

What is the biggest mistake you see in selling naming rights?

"The tendency to under-price. Most naming rights are for perpetuity, but hopefully your institution will grow and its programs will become more popular. Because of these changes, it is important to price on the high end, rather than the low end."

Guidelines Guarantee Consistent Recognition

These guidelines help guarantee consistency of donor recognition for the West Zone Initiative fundraising campaign for Clemson University Athletics (Clemson, SC):

$10,000 – 49,999
Standard signage similar to directional signage materials but still distinguishing in appearance

$50,000 – 149,999
10X12 Plaques only

$150,000 – 249,999
12X14 Plaques & Aluminum/Bronze Lettering (4 in.)

$250,000 – 999,999
Up to 16X16 Plaques & Aluminum/Bronze Lettering (greater than 5 in.)

$1,000,000
20X20 Plaques w/image casting, Aluminum/Bronze Lettering (greater than 5 in.) along with Bronze Lettering on inside façade of WZone Complex

> or = $5,000,000
Name to appear at pinnacle of inside façade of WZone Complex as well as front entrance

CAPITAL CAMPAIGNS AND NAMING OPPORTUNITIES

Arrange Family Events For Named Funds

Philanthropy can and should become a family tradition. In addition to stewarding individuals who have established named funds, be sure to include their family members in your stewardship efforts.

Why not arrange a series of individual family get-togethers to cultivate relationships with family members who may in time choose to add to these funds? Whether you meet for lunch at a local cafe or dinner in the donor's home, use this time to educate and share the impact these funds have on your organization and those you serve.

Here's some of what you might address in a session with family members:

1. When was the fund established, where does the fund currently stand and how has it grown over time?

2. What is the purpose of the fund? What are its unique attributes?

3. What has the fund accomplished since its inception? How has it positively impacted your organization and those you serve?

4. What more could be accomplished if the fund doubled or quadrupled in size over time?

5. How might family members be formally recognized if they add to this fund (or establish named funds of their own)?

How successful you are at organizing these family get-togethers will depend on the willingness and enthusiasm of the original donors to support your efforts. To help make your case, explain to them how such get-togethers will help develop that same philanthropic philosophy they obviously believe is important in future generations.

Offer Major Donors a Script of Naming Options

Helping persons of wealth envision their gifts in action is a crucial step toward turning major gift prospects into donors. For named gifts, in particular, consider offering scripted naming options to enable prospects to determine how a funded project could be worded.

To encourage such gifts to Truman State University (Kirksville, MO), university officials offer naming suggestions that go beyond the individual prospect to honor or memorialize other persons of importance to the donor, says Mark Gambaiana, vice president for university advancement.

For instance, they suggest paying tribute to or memorializing parents, grandparents, children, spouses, other family members, mentors, an organization, business or business associate.

Gambaiana and others at the university also offer prospects examples of how a tribute or memorial naming could be worded:

- Virginia Young Stanton Garden
- Dr. John D. Black Memorial Scholarship
- Stanley & Doris Bohon Family Scholarship
- 79th Field Hospital Scholarship
- Beta Tau Delta/Mary Evelyn Thurman Chemistry Laboratory

The university has established 110 new funds in three years during its $30 million Bright Minds Bright Futures campaign, 70 of which were named, Gambaiana says. Twenty of those named funds were named as memorials or tributes to persons other than the donors. Graduates have honored their professions through the creation of lectureships and speaker series; their parents through endowments for scholarships, student abroad stipends and research fellowships; or honored coaches or professors by naming buildings or scholarships for them.

"Tributes and memorials provide an opportunity to keep major gift conversations moving forward, particularly with individuals who are not interested in attaching their own names to a scholarship, program or facility," says Gambaiana.

Cultivation visits are the key starting point for determining who might be a candidate for making a tribute or memorial naming gift, he says, "In those visits, you need to determine if someone (a faculty member, staff, fellow student, or family member who may or may not have an association with your organization) has made a significant or life-changing impact on the prospect."

Some of the best questions Gambaiana says he uses to uncover that information include:

- What were some of your best experiences as a student here?
- In what positive ways has the university influenced your life?
- How did the university best prepare you for your career?

Source: Mark Gambaiana, Vice President for University Advancement, Truman State University, Kirksville, MO. Phone (660) 785-4133. E-mail: markg@truman.edu

Imaginative Naming Gift Ideas

Always maintain a list of naming gift opportunities — even when you're between capital campaigns — that includes a wide range of gift amounts and types.

Here are examples of creative naming gift possibilities:

- Lounge or lobby.
- Private street, access road or parking structure on your premises.
- Individually endowed parking spaces.
- A supplies acquisition fund.
- An endowed professional development fund for support staff.
- A volunteer work room.

CAPITAL CAMPAIGNS AND NAMING OPPORTUNITIES

Offer One-year Naming Option

Development staff at Connecticut Science Center (Hartford, CT) decided to limit some naming opportunities to one year to ensure that they would always have some naming opportunities to offer, says Ron Katz, director of development.

"We didn't want to limit our ability to raise funds in future years by naming everything in perpetuity," Katz says. "In the early planning stages of our preopening campaign, we spoke with many development directors of established organizations who were left with the legacy of their predecessors — everything was named already."

Plans are to present one-year naming opportunities as ways to visibly recognize a significant annual gift, he says.

Katz and the major gift officer promote one-year naming opportunities mainly through individual conversations with prospects. Offered at the $5,000 to $25,000 level, the options have caught the attention of both corporate donors and individuals. "Corporate donors are looking for something that matches the message they want to present about their business. Individuals just pick something they personally appreciate," he says.

"Our existing annual named gifts are really an outgrowth of conversations with annual and major donors," he says. "We haven't done much in the way of marketing, but rather by judging what donors might like and putting a few options in front of them. We include the list on our website mainly just to catch the interest of someone we might not yet know, or a company looking for a branding opportunity."

Funders of the naming opportunities are recognized on the center's website, with signs on named exhibits and with banners in the center's lobby.

View the naming opportunities at: www.ctsciencecenter.org/support/naming-and-sponsorship.aspx

Source: Ron Katz, Director of Development, Connecticut Science Center, Hartford, CT. Phone (860) 520-2112.
E-mail: rkatz@ctsciencecenter.org

Hospital Offers 'Floors' of Naming Opportunities

To solicit support for a $208 million capital campaign, development staff at Kosair Children's Hospital and Children's Hospital Foundation (Louisville, KY) offer naming opportunities for its facilities, programs, professorships and fellowships.

Donors can name a variety of rooms on the hospital's nine floors, including the emergency/trauma center for $5 million, one of 20 treatment rooms for $25,000 or a child psychiatric annex for $250,000.

Donors have already paid to name the hospital's radiology department and MRI suite.

Donors can also choose to name several programs for gifts of $50,000 to $500,000 or endow several clinical chairs and fellowships for $1 million each. Professorships and fellowships are available for naming with gifts of $270,000 to $500,000, depending on the program and position.

"While some donors aren't interested in naming, others are motivated by other components of the program," says Lynnie Meyer, the foundation's chief development officer. "Naming opportunities can be used as a discussion point for those who do have an interest in naming."

Before setting gift levels, Meyer says, the foundation staff and hospital leadership carefully researched the market and the cost of each project as well as their campaign feasibility study and donor base.

They set naming gift levels at roughly 50 percent of the total cost of each project, based on a rule of thumb they had learned in their research, says Meyer: "It was only used as a guide, however, and adjusted downward based on other information. For example, half of a $20 million project may be $10 million, but if we didn't have that many $10 million donor prospects, we lowered the naming level to $7 million or $8 million so that it would make sense for us."

Once foundation staff and hospital leadership agreed on the ranges, they presented them to the CEO and president, who signed off on them, she says, noting, "It's important to make sure you have institutional support."

For organizations offering naming opportunities, Meyer advises:

❏ Be consistent. Make sure project prices match across the system. Set up credible gift tables. "Don't be desperate and allow someone to name something for far less than what it's worth," she says.

❏ Keep the discussion tied to the case for support and mission. Don't let naming opportunities dominate your dialogue. Concentrate the discussion on how someone can transform something in his or her community. "The majority of people are not making the gift for the naming opportunity," she says, "but rather the impact the program will have on the community as a whole."

Source: Lynnie Meyer, Chief Development Officer, Children's Hospital Foundation, Louisville, KY. Phone (502) 629-8060.
E-mail: lynnie.meyer@nortonhealthcare.org

Major Gift Essentials: Everything You Need to Know to Secure Big Gifts

MAJOR DONOR RECOGNITION AND STEWARDSHIP

Stewardship is often seen as something that follows a gift. Savvy fundraisers, though, know that stewardship (and donor recognition, which is a kind of stewardship) is actually less concerned with the last gift than the next. Put simply, stewardship is a form of cultivation — and one of the most important. For that reason it is a skill that every development professional needs in his or her toolbox.

Organizations Need to Be Careful Stewards

What steps do you take to inform donors how their gifts have been used?

Donors need to be assured that their gifts will be used for the purposes for which they were given or many of them may become disenchanted with your organization and stop making gifts, says John Taylor, associate vice chancellor for advancement services at North Carolina State University (Raleigh, NC).

"Many donors think that organizations don't spend donated funds in the manner for which they were intended," he says.

This perception, says Taylor, goes back to how donors are being informed about how their gifts are being used. This is exacerbated by the fact that donors are hearing in the news that organizations are misusing donors' funds.

"This could easily be fixed by communicating to donors during the course of the expenditure of the funds how those funds are being used," he says.

Source: John Taylor, Associate Vice Chancellor for Advancement Services, North Carolina State University, Raleigh, NC. Phone (919) 513-2954. E-mail: johntaylor@ncsu.edu

Analyze, Acknowledge Cumulative Giving

We tend to pay so much attention to the size of gifts that we sometimes lose sight of those who have remained consistently loyal to our cause, as evidenced by their cumulative giving.

When was the last time you analyzed your list of cumulative donors, those who have given consistently over a 10, 20 or 30-year period?

It doesn't matter whether they gave $25 or $25,000. They're among your most loyal supporters, and that should tell you something.

Consistent, long-term donors:

✓ May be likely to make a major gift if asked and if the project interests them.

✓ Might be among your most likely ambassadors. Invite them to become involved in some capacity of friend-raising and fund development.

✓ Deserve to be recognized in special ways. Start a special club or society based on long-term cumulative giving. Publicly recognize these donors.

Provide Customized, Individual Stewardship

Jay Goulart, executive director of advancement at Ridley College (St. Catherine's, Ontario, Canada), eliminated traditional major donor stewardship such as annual reports in favor of customized, individual stewardship.

"For many organizations, the average method for recognizing donors is an annual report," Goulart says. "But the moment you write something for everyone, it's not for anyone. We are all asking for money. The place where a nonprofit has the opportunity to stand out is in the donor's experience between donations."

For a visit to a donor family underwriting a student's education, Goulart had his internal staff create a video that included the student addressing the donor about how his/her support has impacted the student's education. "I pulled out my iPad, loaded the video, and brought to life what their money is making happen," he says.

While building a new facility, Goulart's staff put out a stewardship piece containing images and video, so donors could watch the building as it was built. They broadcast the building's grand opening event live, with streaming video on the Internet.

"It's about taking the intangible and creating a way for people to touch it," Goulart says. "It is that ingenuity that will allow nonprofits to compete. Making the decision to donate rewarding, and encouraging continuing support with communications about what they've accomplished, will increase a nonprofit's ability to grow a donor to a higher giving level."

Source: Jay Goulart, Executive Director of Advancement, Ridley College, St. Catherine's, Ontario, Canada. Phone (905) 684-1889, ext 2244. E-mail: jay_goulart@ridleycollege.edu

Regularly Review Your Top 100 Individual Prospects

Your top 100 prospects represent a dynamic, ever-changing group of individuals.

To properly rank and steward this important group, review your list regularly — at least monthly — and prioritize who should remain, who should be added and who should be moved.

Include in this review process criteria related to both capability and inclination to give.

Give staff and highly involved board members a list of your current top prospects, along with additional names not presently on that list. Instruct those persons to first review the list individually, assigning a rating of 1, 2 or 3 beside each prospect's name — 1 meaning keep on the list, 2 meaning discuss for possible change in status, and 3 meaning recommend adding to the list.

Then, meet as a group and compare your thoughts.

MAJOR DONOR RECOGNITION AND STEWARDSHIP

Create Policy for Publicizing Momentous Gifts As First Step in Stewarding Donors

Seek Donor Direction When Publicizing Momentous Gifts

When promoting a major gift, structure gift announcements according to donor specifications, says Wendy Walker Zeller, director of donor relations and communications for Washburn Endowment Association, the fundraising arm of Washburn University (Topeka, KS). By properly publicizing major gifts with your donor's wishes in mind, you are letting the donor know how important his/her gift is while increasing the possibility of the donor making another gift at a later date, says Zeller.

"What the donor wants is foremost in our minds," Zeller says. "If they are unsure, we offer suggestions based on the intention of the gift."

Make the gift announcement event pleasing and rewarding for the donor by meeting his/her needs and expectations, says Zeller. Washburn staff work directly with donors to create the experience the donors would like to have at the gift announcement, she says. If a donor will not be present for the announcement, she says, they ask for the donor's input and then share the details of the plan with the donor.

"We try to make the experience a good one for the media as well, keeping in mind the best time of day and most comfortable location to hold a press conference," she says, "ensuring we have adequate lighting and sound and giving access to the donor for questions."

When possible, says Zeller, they also prepare a press packet for the media that contains background information for the story.

News releases announcing major gifts are sent to a broad media list, including media outlets that reflect the donor's personal history such as the donor's hometown.

Source: Wendy Walker Zeller, Director of Donor Relations & Communications, Washburn Endowment Association, Topeka, KS. Phone (785) 670-4483. E-mail: wwalker@wea.org

Take inspiration from these two organizations to publicize your next major gift:

Share Announcement With Those Who Will Benefit From It Most

Washburn University (Topeka, KS) recently received its largest single gift from an individual — a $5 million gift from Trish and Richard Davidson to supplement faculty salaries in its School of Business.

To publicize the momentous gift, Washburn officials turned to the university policy that calls for all gift announcements to be structured to the donor's specifications, says Wendy Walker Zeller, director of donor relations and communications for the Washburn Endowment Association, Washburn University's fundraising arm.

The Davidsons wanted to be present for this gift announcement, Zeller says, "so we spent a great deal of time working out the details to meet their wishes." The Davidsons asked to speak to a class of business students. Also attending the class were the news media, along with the university president, endowment association president, business school dean and board of regents chair. The 100-some students were invited to stay for the gift announcement, which took place just after the press arrived in the classroom.

Media received press packets featuring the Davidsons' biography and were seated at the front of the classroom. A backdrop with the university logo and drape displaying the business school were arranged for the announcement.

"The students gave a spontaneous standing ovation following the announcement, which was filmed by a couple of the local TV stations," she says.

"Other than a few people on campus and several trustees, we kept the gift amount and identity of the donors under wraps until the official announcement, which helped build suspense and pique press interest," she says.

Carefully Time Release of News to Maximize Publicity, Impact

Chatham Hall (Chatham, VA), an independent college-preparatory high school for girls, recently received a $31 million gift from the estate of Elizabeth Beckwith Nilsen, a former student. The gift was the largest single gift to any girls' independent school.

Because of the magnitude of the gift, Melissa Evans Fountain, director of the office of advancement, says they followed this special plan of action in publicizing it:

On announcement day, classes were delayed until 9:30 a.m. From 8 to 9 a.m., the president of the board and head of school announced the gift to the faculty and answered questions about the gift. At 9 a.m., faculty were joined by the staff and students, and the head of school and board president announced the gift to this larger group.

Staff sent a news release at 9:15 a.m. through US 1 Premium Newswire, the Philanthropy Microlist and the Education Microlist and posted it on the school's website.

At 9:30 a.m., after the all-school meeting, the head of Chatham Hall sent an e-mail announcing the gift to all major educational associations, suggesting they share the news with their constituents.

From 9:30 to 10:30 a.m., calls were made to members of the Alumnae Council and Parent Advisory Council, past heads of the school, certain major donors and other VIPs (all trustees and several top donors knew about the gift prior to the announcement).

At 10:30 a.m. an e-mail blast was sent to all constituents in the school's database and the announcement was posted on the school's Facebook page.

That same day, college officials mailed a press release to donor prospects with a cover letter announcing the gift in the context of the school's capital campaign. They also sent the press release to state and local VIPs, area leaders in the Episcopal Church and an admission office list that included prospective students and educational consultants. A special article was also written for the school's fall 2009 alumnae magazine.

Sources: Melissa Evans Fountain, Director of the Office of Advancement, Chatham Hall, Chatham, VA. Phone (434) 432-5549. E-mail: mfountain@chathamhall.org
Wendy Walker Zeller, Director of Donor Relations & Communications, Washburn Endowment Association, Topeka, KS. Phone (785) 670-4483. E-mail: wwalker@wea.org

MAJOR DONOR RECOGNITION AND STEWARDSHIP

Share Impact of Existing Endowed Gifts

Do you provide a formal yearly update to persons who have established endowed funds with your organization? Informing these donors of the status of their particular funds and those funds' impact should be a must for two reasons: It's a good stewardship practice, and doing so could very easily lead to donors adding more to established funds.

Meet one-on-one with those who have set up endowed funds to:

1. **Review the current progress of your organization's overall endowment for the past year.** Who is managing your endowment? Did the fund grow? At what rate? Were there any changes in your endowment's investment policy?

2. **Review the individual's established endowment fund.** What was the amount of annual interest used to underwrite the program for which the fund was established? What rate of return was made available and how was it calculated?

3. **Explain how the funds were used?** If the endowed fund was a scholarship, for instance, who were the recipients and how much did each receive? Give the donor a solid sense of how the gift is having a positive impact on those you serve.

4. **Help the donor extend his/her understanding of the endowed fund to a higher level.** Paint a picture of what more could be accomplished were more funds added to the endowment, either through outright gifts, a planned gift or both. Do so in a way, however, that doesn't undercut what has already been contributed.

5. **Leave the donor with a written summary of your presentation.** Give him/her a document to review.

This formal update and stewardship procedure will make the donor more aware that his/her fund is a living gift that continues to impact your cause yearly.

Towers of Old Main Giving Society Aims at $100,000 Gifts

At the University of Arkansas (Fayetteville, AR), The Towers of Old Main giving society provides a way to thank and recognize its most generous benefactors.

Once donors reach the $100,000 cumulative giving level, university officials invite them to be recognized as Towers of Old Main. Nearly 600 persons have done so since the program began in 2000, says Danielle Strickland, director of development communications. Recognition is optional, Strickland says. "Every benefactor is different. Some prefer to keep their contributions private, and others are open to the recognition."

Every other spring, school officials host a black-tie event to induct members into the program, with the chancellor and system president presenting them with a Towers of Old Main medallion. Members also receive pins based on giving levels: a silver pin for $500,000; a gold pin for $1 million; and a ruby pin for $5 million.

Towers of Old Main benefactors are invited to special events throughout the year, says Strickland. "They are, of course, some of the most valued members of the Arkansas family."

Members also receive donor-centered newsletters and e-mails to further engage them in university activities.

For organizations considering such a recognition program, Kris Macechko, director of the Towers of Old Main program, suggests assembling a task force of major donors to help establish criteria and recognition guidelines. That process "gave our donors ownership from the start," Macechko says. "It's also important to research carefully the ramifications of establishing

a giving society and have a clear understanding of the society's purpose."

The program director says the planning process should address these key questions:

- Who will manage the society?
- Is it a membership organization or a recognition organization?
- How will people be notified of their qualification?
- Will there be levels of giving (recognition) within the society?
- Will publications (pamphlets, for example) be needed to share with members or potential members?
- How will the society be funded?
- What will the society be named?

Macechko notes that university officials are reviewing the program and may make some language changes. She says some people want to replace "membership" wording with "recognition" for giving. "For example, donors do not have to be inducted to be members of Towers; they simply have to accept the chancellor's offer to be recognized."

Sources: Kris Macechko, Director Constituent Relations; Danielle Strickland, Director of Development Communications; University of Arkansas, Fayetteville, AR. Phone (479) 575-7200 (Strickland) or (479) 575-7346 (Macechko).
E-mail: kmacech@uark.edu or strick@uark.edu.
Website: http://advancement.uark.edu/rd_vcad/giving/240.php

MAJOR DONOR RECOGNITION AND STEWARDSHIP

Gallery of Honor Showcases Donors

Consider creating a recognition wall to permanently honor your major donors.

Since 2004, persons who give $5,000 or more to Carroll Hospital Center (Westminster, MD) have had their names placed on its Gallery of Honor, a 20-foot wide, five-foot tall recognition wall located in the most visible spot in the hospital — the outer lobby.

Sherri Hosfeld Joseph, director of development, says they created the display to encourage donors' giving and inspire them to give more and reach to achieve a higher level on the display. Cumulative giving amounts are based on gifts made since 1989, which she says is as far back as the foundation's electronic records go.

"We make sure our consistent donors are aware of the wall, and let new donors know that a gift at a certain level will get them on the wall," she says. "We also place brochures in a rack by the wall so visitors can grab one if they are interested in knowing how to make a gift."

The honor wall recognizes eight giving levels:

1. Chairman's Circle, $1 million or more
2. Sinnott Fellows, $500,000 to $999,999
3. President's Club, $250,000 to $499,999
4. 1961 Society, $100,000 to $249,999
5. Stewards Club, $50,000 to $99,999
6. Galen Club, $25,000 to $49,999
7. Sponsor, $10,000 to $24,999
8. Patron, $5,000 to $9,999

When donors make gifts that move them up a giving level, Hosfeld Joseph says, development staff place new name plaques in the appropriate giving spots, then send the old plaques to the donors as a gift, along with an invitation to come see the gallery. Donors who include the hospital in estate plans are honored on the wall under a Bridge Builders listing.

Development staff add names to the wall twice a year by running a cumulative giving report of $5,000-plus, says Hosfeld Joseph. The magnetic plaques, engraved with donors' names, cost $25 to $80, depending on the size.

Source: Sherri Hosfeld Joseph, Director of Development, Carroll Hospital Center & Carroll Hospice, Westminster, MD. Phone (410) 871-6200. E-mail: Sjoseph@carrollhospitalcenter.org

Invite a Donor to Your Staff Meeting

As part of regular staff meetings, why not invite a donor to come and share insight into a particular topic such as what motivated him/her to make a gift?

Inviting a donor to meet with your staff has multiple benefits, among them:

1. Both staff and donor benefit from face to face contact, associating names and faces.

2. The donor receives a unique honor being invited into your office as a special guest offering advice on a specific topic.

3. This simple stewardship act serves to involve the donor in a new and different way. His/her presence will provide a greater appreciation of the overall development function and its importance in your organization.

4. Your staff will discover even more about the donor — motivations, likes/dislikes — that will surely be helpful in the realization of future gifts. You may even identify additional ways in which the donor could become involved with your organization.

5. The thoughts and advice shared by the donor may help in future fundraising efforts.

Content not available in this edition

Prominently featured in the outer lobby of Carroll Hospital Center (Westminster, MD), this donor wall recognizes persons who make cumulative gifts of $5,000 and more.

Major Gift Essentials: Everything You Need to Know to Secure Big Gifts

BUILDING A FUNDRAISING BOARD

It is no exaggeration to say that board members set the tone for the entirety of an organization's fundraising operations. An engaged and capable board gives generously (sometimes up to 60 percent of a major campaign) and provides a compelling example for other major donors to follow. It is worth your time to make sure you have a competent board filled with members who are both givers and getters.

Build a Board of Major Givers

It doesn't matter whether your organization is relatively new or has existed for some time, if you want to generate major gifts it's important to build a board of directors — over time — able and willing to set an example for others.

When a charity has a capable board in place, it's not uncommon for the board's collective giving to amount to as much as 30 to 60 percent of a capital campaign goal.

What about those who are committed to your cause and willing to give of their time? Provide opportunities for involvement for these valued patrons, but limit board membership to those who can make meaningful financial gifts.

Recognizing that transforming a board takes time, here are some strategies to build board giving:

1. Recruit board members who know they are expected to contribute a minimum amount each year. Hint: The higher your expectations, the more interest you will receive from those most capable.

2. Put your most affluent board member in charge of assisting you in recruiting others of affluence.

3. Don't tolerate board members who don't meet expectations. Ask them to step down. It's as simple as that.

4. Ask your model board donors to challenge the rest of the board.

5. Publicize exemplary board gifts as much as you can. Not only will you be cultivating the donor toward the realization of another, even larger gift, you will also be encouraging other board members to follow suit.

Strengthen Board Member Solicitation Skills

Board member solicitation can make or break fundraising efforts for one simple reason, says Jim Lyons, senior partner at Pride Philanthropy (Alpharetta, GA): Board members are five to 10 times more likely to get appointments with potential donors than development staff are.

"It's easy to turn down a professional fundraiser; their job is to get turned down," Lyons says. "But when a volunteer who is giving their own money to an organization calls and says, 'This is really important, and I'd like to tell you about it,' people will usually make time to listen."

Lyons answers questions about creating effective board member solicitors:

What is the biggest obstacle to effective board member fundraising?

"It often goes back to how they were recruited. All too often we are so focused on recruiting toward yes that we end up down-playing critical fundraising expectations. It gets us board members, but it sets our organizations up for failure."

How should fundraising expectations be communicated to potential or new board members?

"They need to be told there are different ways to help. Some people are good at identifying prospects, some are good at telling an organization's story, and some don't want to set up appointments or take hard questions, but are willing to look someone in the eye and make the ask. No one has to do all three, but all board members should know that they are expected to be contributing in at least one area."

How should development staff assist in board member solicitation?

"They should first of all help board members develop a prospect list of three to five contacts. They should prepare the meeting materials, should expect to do much of the follow up, and can, according to the board member's preference, attend meetings to answer detail questions and supply statistics. But they should never set up the meeting. If a staff member calls to make an appointment on someone's behalf, it defeats the whole purpose."

What should board members know about closing solicitations?

"There are three keys. First, make sure you always ask for a specific amount. When you offer a range, people will always migrate to the bottom end. Second, when you have made the ask, just be quiet. It can be hard to sit through the silence, but if you start talking, you'll often be talking them out of the gift. Last, make sure there is a specific follow-up plan that leaves the ball in your court — something like 'I understand this is a big decision. Tell me when you would like us to follow up with you.'"

What should be included in training to build board members' solicitation skills?

"It's nice to have a meeting strictly devoted to solicitation training. You will want to do some role play and practice in the meeting — pair everyone up so they are not performing in front of each other, but have each member play both the solicitor and the donor. People will resist, but they always say it was helpful after the fact."

How do you establish an ongoing culture of board member fundraising?

"It starts at the top. It needs to be an ongoing CEO message and an important part of board member orientation and training. It's a process that takes time. You can't just send a memo and say you've established a culture of philanthropy. It requires long-term commitment."

Source: Jim Lyons, Senior Partner, Pride Philanthropy, Alpharetta, GA. Phone (888) 417-0707. E-mail: Pride1jim@aol.com. Website: www.pridephilanthropy.com

BUILDING A FUNDRAISING BOARD

Help Board Members Realize Their Potential

Knowing that as much as 60 percent of a capital campaign goal can be realized through current and former board members' gifts, what are you doing to help individual board members realize their potential as transformational donors — those whose gifts could literally transform your organization?

Cultivate board members toward the realization of transformational gifts by:

- Sharing examples of others who have made such gifts to other charities. Demonstrate the before and after of such gifts.

- Developing a strategic plan — with their involvement — that creates a lofty vision of what could be with the proper level of support.

- Involving them in the identification, cultivation and/ or solicitation of someone capable of making a transformational gift.

Accountability Form Improves Board Member Giving

A simple form is boosting board member accountability and giving for the Make-A-Wish Foundation of the Mid-South (Memphis, TN).

Liz Larkin, president/CEO, says the board commitment contract (shown below) has helped to significantly increase board gifts. In 2004, before implementing the form, Larkin says, only three of 14 board members gave at the wish sponsorship level ($5,000 and up). Today, 13 of the 14 give at least $5,000 annually.

Larkin collected forms from other Make-A-Wish chapters and, with three members of the board development committee, created the document to address their organization's specific needs. Now, board members are required to sign the form at the start of each fiscal year. Board member prospects are informed of this annual responsibility prior to their being voted on to join the board.

In signing the form, board members are committing to "The Give" (donating $5,000 per board member), "The Get" (soliciting direct support gifts from individuals, corporations, foundations, etc. to help offset daily operating expenses) and event support (agreeing to attend, raise sponsors, pledges, auction items and/or sell tickets for at least one of the organization's major events).

Larkin tracks members' progress with a board report card shared at board meetings that details how close they are to meeting their annual commitments to give funds and get support, as well as meeting attendance, fundraising help, board member recruitment, etc.

"If a board member is not meeting the expectations of giving their time, talents and treasures, then the board chair has a conversation with them," she says. "Typically, the board member will either resign or step up. The board members like the accountability."

Source: Liz Larkin, President/CEO, Make-A-Wish Foundation of the Mid-South, Memphis, TN. Phone (901) 680-9474. E-mail: llarkin@midsouth. wish.org

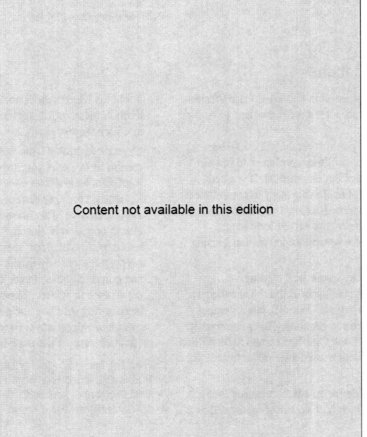

Content not available in this edition

Seven Ways to Boost Board Member Fundraising

The well-worn adage of "time, talent and treasure" is insufficient for the demands of modern fundraising, says Justin Tolan, chief fundraising adviser at the nonprofit consultancy ME&V (Cedar Falls, IA). "Donors are more savvy than ever, and board members absolutely have to lead by giving, at least to the degree to which they are capable."

Tolan shares seven ways to boost board member fundraising, both giving and getting:

1. **Clarity in recruitment.** If you expect board members to be active fundraisers, make that clear in the recruitment process, says Tolan. "You can't wait until the end of the year or start of a capital campaign to tell new members that you expect 100 percent board participation."

2. **Minimum giving.** Further clarify expectations with annual board commitment agreements of at least the nonprofit's minimum club level. Board members' presence in a legacy society will also strengthen requests for planned gifts.

3. **Campaign giving goals.** Goals and stretch goals for board giving in capital campaigns promote board giving, says Tolan. Be specific. "Setting numeric goals like raising $100,000 from your board's 20 members gives a very clear sense of individual obligation."

4. **Board expansion.** One simple way to increase board giving is to increase board size. Larger boards amplify fundraising potential while enhancing governance by allowing groups of members to specialize in areas such as publicity or fundraising.

5. **Thank-a-thon.** For boards with a weak culture of fundraising, Tolan says a thank-a-thon can be a great first step. Create a list of all donors from the past three months and have board members take turns making thank-you calls.

6. **Fundraising committee.** A dedicated fundraising committee can sharpen board members' attention to the issue, he says. Have the committee submit regular reports, put those reports at the beginning of the agenda and celebrate all levels of success.

7. **Cleaning house.** It's never too late to start building strong giving habits, but it might be too late for certain individuals, says Tolan. Replacing board members who have no history of annual giving and no desire to give to capital campaigns with more involved supporters can transform a board and, ultimately, a nonprofit.

Source: Justin Tolan, Chief Fundraising Adviser, ME&V, Cedar Falls, IA. Phone (319) 268-9151. E-mail: jtolan@MEandV.com. Website: www.MEandV.com

Publicize Board Donations

Earlier this year, several trustees on the board at Case Western Reserve University (Cleveland, OH) gave more than $6 million to their school.

While the trustees knew publicizing the gift could benefit Case's fundraising efforts, some of them preferred to remain anonymous. So the trustees and development staff worked together to create a specialized leadership story to communicate the gift as a symbol of their strength as an organization overall, rather than focusing on the generosity of the individuals.

This technique illuminates several important fundraising issues:

✓ **Promote board gifts; they speak well of your organization.** Such gifts instill confidence, so use them to encourage other trustees to give. Case officials reiterated past instances of board giving, reminding their community that since fiscal year 2008-09, Case had earned $108 million in fundraising, much of which came after major trustee gift announcements.

✓ **Tailor gift response to donor needs.** Remember that gift publicity is an important form of stewardship, as well as publicity. Meet with donors to determine how to recognize them in meaningful, appropriate ways that highlight areas in which they're giving.

✓ **Create continuity.** This donor-specific approach requires careful tracking of your project's progress. Case's Amy Raufman, head of development communications, and Lara Kalafatis, vice president of university relations, emphasize the importance of archiving your work with donors even after a donation is closed. "The donor needs to see the relationship with your institution as unified," Kalafatis says. One way to do this is to integrate development and communication teams for a streamlined full-service experience in which a donor's needs are more likely to be fully met. At Case, the position of director of donor communications was created specifically to manage communications with donors and media.

Source: Amy Raufman, Head of Development Communications, and Lara Kalafatis, Vice President of University Relations, Case Western Reserve University, Cleveland, OH. Phone (216) 368-0547. E-mail: aer35@case.edu (Raufman). Website: www.case.edu

BUILDING A FUNDRAISING BOARD

Invite Board Members to Introduce You and Your Cause

Do you have a method to encourage board members to introduce you and your organization to individuals, businesses and foundations?

If your board is made up of movers and shakers, they should be in positions to help introduce your organization and assist in prospect cultivation. And for those board members who shudder at the thought of asking people for money, you can assure them that their primary role is simply to help make introductions and cultivate friendships. You or another advancement official can be prepared to make any asks.

Formalize your procedure for involving board members in this friend-making process by developing a form similar to the example shown. At a scheduled board meeting, ask board members to complete it and return it to you within a specified number of days. Then be prepared to begin following up with each board member immediately. (It's important to act while the assignment is still fresh in their minds.)

When you distribute the form, be sure to include your last honor roll of contributors so board members will be sure not to include names of those who are presently contributing to your organization. Better yet, also include a list of nondonors who would be likely prospect candidates.

FRIEND-MAKING OBJECTIVES FOR BOARD MEMBERS
~Confidential~

The purpose of this project is to involve all board members in making introductions and cultivating relationships with non-donors capable of making gifts of $10,000 or more. Your ability to help establish a positive relationship with friends and associates will help broaden our base of future major gift support as we plan for the future.

Our goal is to make individual introductory visits with each person you have identified within the next three months. Subsequent visits and objectives will be determined once initial calls have been completed.

Please identify three or more prospects (individuals, businesses or foundations) — who are presently not donors — capable of contributing $10,000 or more to our organization. We ask that you complete this form within the next week and return it to [Name].

Once your form is received, a development officer will contact you to begin coordinating available dates and times to set appointments with the persons you have identified.

Your Name _____ Date _____
1. Prospect _____ _____
Your Relationship to the Prospect: _____
Helpful Background Information (e.g., occupation, title, source of wealth): _____
2. Prospect _____
Your Relationship to the Prospect: _____
Helpful Background Information: _____
3. Prospect _____
Your Relationship to the Prospect: _____
Helpful Background Information: _____

Stay Connected With Former Board Members

Developing strong relationships with current board members is key to staying connected with them — and keeping them engaged with and supporting your organization — after they retire.

"There is a greater chance of keeping former board members engaged if they were developed and cultivated during their tenure on the board," says Diane Dean, principal, The Dean Consulting Group (Rutherford, NJ). "There is a unique advantage to having informed insight regarding board members' interests, talents, skills and reasons for committing to the organization on a volunteer leadership level."

Tools to develop and sustain relationships include personal questionnaires, self-assessments and committee evaluations, plus activities at orientations and board retreats.

Forming a board development committee to recruit, engage and develop board members is another useful strategy.

"The best board strategies, the ones that get results that can be tracked to prove success, are those that are incorporated as programs with written procedures and a clear goal of what success looks like," says Paul Nazareth, manager of planned and personal giving, Catholic Archdiocese of Toronto (Toronto,

Ontario, Canada).

A well-crafted communications plan should include a formal recognition process for people coming on and off the board.

"One innovative idea I've seen is an organization that will add a 'recommendation' to a board member's LinkedIn profile if he or she fulfills the top five criteria of an excellent board member (make a commitment to the board, volunteer in programs, advocate in the community, network for the organization, make a leadership or planned gift)," Nazareth says.

One way to engage retiring board members, that is often overlooked, is to simply ask them what level of involvement they would like and whether that involvement would occur immediately after the end of their board service or in a few years.

Sources: Diane D. Dean, Principal, The Dean Consulting Group, Rutherford, NJ. Phone (800) 686-1975. E-mail: ddean@ thedeanconsultinggroup.com. Website: www.thedeanconsultinggroup.com Paul Nazareth, Manager, Planned and Personal Giving at Catholic Archdiocese of Toronto, Toronto, Ontario, Canada. Phone (416) 934-3411. E-mail: pnazareth@archtoronto.org. Website: www.archtoronto.org

BUILDING A FUNDRAISING BOARD

Groom a Board Member Recruiter

If your board could use some beefing up — based on capacity to give — why not assign that duty to one existing board member who can make a long-term difference?

Meet with your best recruiter choice and explain that, over the next three years, you intend to add new board members who have the capacity to make major gifts. Share with the recruiter the gift range you have in mind.

Ask the board member to help identify, research and cultivate relationships with persons who fit your criteria for board members. Meet monthly or quarterly with the board member to review names and map out plans to introduce your organization to would-be board members. Once you and the board member feel right about a particular prospect, feed that person's name to your board nominating committee for consideration.

Leverage the Powerful Reputations of Your Board Members

Board members articulate strategic direction, provide organizational continuity and often supply their share of elbow grease to a nonprofit's mission. But beyond the services they provide, their reputation in the local, regional or national community can be of great benefit as well.

Larry Stybel understands how boards operate inside and out. He is co-founder and vice president of Board Options, Inc. (Boston, MA) — a nationally recognized company specializing in helping boards be effective problem-solving units through the application of practical behavioral science — and executive in residence at the Sawyer School of Business at Suffolk University (Boston, MA).

Here, Stybel shares his expertise in the art of leveraging the reputation of prestigious board members:

What is the central rationale behind showcasing well-known board members?

"Donors, when they were children, were told by their mothers that they would be known by the company they keep. This is what board members do for nonprofits. If you are an upcoming nonprofit that does not have top-flight status, one way to create reputation and cache is through your board members. In branded institutions like MIT or Princeton, the institution gives luster to the board member. But in smaller organizations, the opposite is true: board members lend their credibility to the nonprofit."

So in attracting donors and other prospective board members...

"Prestigious board members function like the anchor store of a shopping center, the place that all the other shops cluster around. If a brand-name person is on your board, other people will want to be associated with that individual, and, by extension, your organization and its mission."

Are there any challenges to having well-known board members?

"If you are not a prestigious institution, there is a limit to how many brand-name people you can afford to have on your board. Two is great; six might not be so great. One of the disadvantages of bright star board members is that they often have only limited time to put into your organization. They will not typically be the 'shirtsleeves' board members who dig in and really get things done. Bright stars are important, but they are prone to fighting with each other, and too many can be counterproductive."

What should organizations know about using the name of a bright star board member?

"That it should always be done with the knowledge and agreement of the board member. That individual is lending his or her name and stature to your organization, and you don't want to abuse that privilege. A bright star should never find out you used his name after the fact. And also be aware that if he is a CEO or president, his business will often want to clear the use of the name beforehand as well."

Is there anything a shirtsleeves-heavy board should do or not do in looking for bright star members?

"One tip is to make board participation a finite commitment. Prestigious individuals don't want to be trapped on the board of a smaller nonprofit forever, even if they believe in its mission. Setting a term limit of two or three years spares them the awkwardness of resigning and makes them more likely to agree to the initial commitment."

Source: Larry Stybel, Co-founder and Vice President, Board Options, Inc., Boston, MA. Phone (617) 594-7627. E-mail: Lstybel@boardoptions.com

Major Gift Essentials: Everything You Need to Know to Secure Big Gifts

HIGH-DOLLAR GIFT CLUBS AND GIVING SOCIETIES

Gift clubs can play an important role in major gift programs. The companionship they offer satisfies a natural desire for belonging, while their high-dollar thresholds supply the kind of exclusivity to which many major donors are accustomed. Giving societies do raise funds directly, but more importantly, they offer a means to identify, cultivate and steward major prospects. Use the following tips and strategies to get the most out of your giving club.

Review Others' Top Gift Clubs To Refine Your Own

What's your organization's top giving club or level for annual gifts? How do the benefits of contributing at that level differ from lower-level giving? How do donor benefits from your top gift level differ from those of other nonprofits' most prestigious gift clubs?

Your most generous annual giving donors will obviously be top candidates when it comes to seeking major gifts. That's why it's important to keep expanding that pool. To do so, your top giving level (or club) should be perceived as one to which everyone wants to belong.

Look at the nonprofits throughout your community. Many have prestigious membership levels for those who give at, say, the $1,000-and-above level. Which nonprofits enjoy the greatest number of donors at that level? Which are perceived to be the most prestigious groups?

To refine your own top gift club, learn and evaluate what others are doing by:

1. Picking up literature from other nonprofits to see how they market their top gift club and determine what benefits they offer donors at that level.

2. Finding out who, among your donor constituency, also gives generously to other nonprofit groups. Visit with them to gain insight into their perceptions of other nonprofits' top giving groups. What do they find most appealing about them? What do they least like? What events do they make a point to attend and why?

3. Conducting a focus group discussion — or distributing a survey — with a handful of your donors who are presently contributing at your top level. Ask them questions that reveal perceptions about your current club benefits.

Annual Giving Societies Attract $1,000-plus Donors

Children's Healthcare of Atlanta (Atlanta, GA) has two annual leadership giving societies for $1,000-plus donors: Hope's Circle for female donors and Will's Club for male donors.

Hope's Circle, started five years ago, has nearly 250 members. Will's Club, started about a year ago with about 25 donors, has nearly tripled in size to almost 70 members.

Both are opt-in, meaning members are not automatically enrolled, but must agree to join, says Elesha Mavrommatis, development officer. "The opt-in feature helps us identify donors who want to be contacted on a regular basis," she says. "In effect, they self-identify as being open to a call from a development officer."

Hope's Circle members receive a monthly e-newsletter as well as invitations to behind-the-scenes tours, roundtable discussions with physicians, luncheons and other donor events. Will's Club members receive a quarterly e-newsletter and invitations to member-hosted events. Both groups are recognized in the organization's community report, on signage at the hospitals and on the medical facility's website.

"While Hope's Circle is staff-driven — I coordinate tours and events — Will's Club is member-driven," says Mavrommatis. "Will's Club members plan their own events and are more active recruiters for the group. For the men, it's a way to socialize with other men who want to support the hospital. I believe that long-term, the men's group will be successful, because they feel ownership of it." Events organized by the men's group to date include skeet shooting, a wine tasting and a tour and tasting at a local brewery.

Mavrommatis says switching giving society membership due dates from anniversary date to calendar year has made tracking membership much easier. For example, members who give in 2009 are recognized as 2009 donors and have all of 2010 to make a qualifying gift for the next fiscal year.

The giving societies are promoted in the organization's annual fund brochure and on its website, and information about the groups is communicated to major gift officers and corporate gift officers who might have donors who would qualify as members but who may not make a gift directly through the annual fund.

When a qualifying gift comes in through the annual fund, staff send an acknowledgement that includes the opportunity to join the giving society and how to do so.

"When we call them to thank them for their gift, we will also mention it again," she says. "Once they join Hope's Circle, we call to welcome them and send them the last e-newsletter that went out, which includes my contact information sent under my e-mail address. This helps me develop a relationship with these donors."

Will's Club communicates almost exclusively through e-mail.

At Thanksgiving, Mavrommatis sends handwritten cards to all Hope's Circle members. The same happens for Will's Club members. Hope's Circle and Will's Club members also receive a holiday card by e-mail, activities she says help develop a relationship with these donors, which is an important element in the success of the giving societies.

Source: Elesha Mavrommatis, Development Officer, Children's Healthcare of Atlanta, Atlanta, GA. Phone (404) 785-7336. E-mail: Elesha.Mavrommatis@choa.org

HIGH-DOLLAR GIFT CLUBS AND GIVING SOCIETIES

Acknowledge Donors In Unique Ways

Q. **What unique ways are you acknowledging your planned giving donors?**

"One of the member benefits for our Benedictine Legacy Society is a Saint John's Estate Planning Binder. This binder has an embossed cover showing our Abbey Church, a major architectural touch point. It has plastic sleeves for holding documents related to a donor's estate plans, such as trust documents, will, advisor's contact information, etc. Each section has a log for noting the latest information additions.

"Some donors use it as the basic storage for their papers and keep it in a secure location. Others put photocopies of documents in the sleeves with notes describing the location of the original documents. We very strongly recommend that originals be placed in safety deposit boxes or other secure locations.

"Many donors have expressed appreciation for the usefulness of the book in two ways: It reminds them of what documents are important and also provides a copy of the documents for heirs to use to identify originals."

—Jim Dwyer, Director of Planned Giving, Saint John's University and Abbey (Collegeville, MN)

Use Retirees Club to Utilize Seasoned Ambassadors

To better engage potential donors, create inititiaves that reach specific groups in personalized ways they can appreciate and enjoy.

At Illinois Wesleyan University (IWU), Bloomington, IL, communications staff take extra steps to reach a valuable group of stakeholders — retirees — by sponsoring the Retirees Coffee Club at the campus student center.

"Our faculty are great representatives for the institution in the local community, often helping us to identify potential issues and advocating for us when an issue arises," says Matt Kurz, IWU vice president for public relations. "They also form very close bonds with their students, and quite often those relationships last for many years, so retired faculty can really be important in the alumni relations and development areas."

In offering the coffee club, Kurz says, IWU staff hope to send the message to retirees that "while they're gone, they are not forgotten." He recommends developing a similar program "if there is a fit with the organizational culture, as there is here at Wesleyan."

Source: Matt Kurz, Vice President for Public Relations, Illinois Wesleyan University, Bloomington, IL. Phone (309) 556-3203. E-mail: mkurz@iwu.edu. Website: www.iwu.edu

Major Donor Club Helps University Raise Major Gifts

The University of Tennessee (UT) (Knoxville, TN) Development Council consists of approximately 70 major donors, each of whom has contributed more than $100,000 to a UT department or unit.

"Development council members are interested in being more engaged with the university and want to interact with administration at the presidential and board-of-trustee level," says Suzy Garner, director of development. "They are generous, passionate about UT (specifically those areas which they support), and want to be advocates."

Each member makes an annual gift of $1,000 to fund the council's meeting activities and the annual awards dinner, where UT's highest awards are presented, including the Development Council Service Award, the Philanthropist(s) of the Year Award and Haslam Presidential Medal.

The group meets formally twice a year. Between meetings, members participate in various activities, such as touring campus facilities made possible with private donations, interacting with faculty and students, assisting with solicitations of other alumni or friends, talking with their state representatives who direct funds to UT, hosting regional campaign events and making recommendations regarding potential prospects.

New members are recruited through current members' recommendations. Development staff is asked to make formal nominations. Garner says that most members live in Tennessee because that is where UT's highest concentration of donors are, but they encourage participation from across the country.

To keep members engaged and participating in the council, Garner says, they work hard to respond to members' feedback — whether that is making changes to meeting schedules or program content. "Many of our members go on to serve UT in other ways, such as on the UT Foundation Board and the Board of Trustees. We want them to feel like insiders and encourage as much presidential and trustee interaction as possible. Also, we try not to take up so much of their time that they can't continue to help those areas at UT about which they are most passionate."

Source: Suzy Garner, Director of Development, The University of Tennessee, Knoxville, TN. Phone (865) 974-2115. E-mail: suzy.garner@tennessee.edu

HIGH-DOLLAR GIFT CLUBS AND GIVING SOCIETIES

Cater Renewal Efforts To Higher-Level Donors

By nature of their level of support, major donors have a definite distinction from persons who make smaller gifts. Your strategies for renewing major gifts should be distinctive too. The following steps can help you get there:

✓ For your most generous donors, any renewal conversation should be handled in person. If this is not possible, at a minimum they should be contacted by phone.

✓ When contacting your other major donors, make sure that letters are personal in nature and personalized. They should not receive form letters. Any written correspondence should carry an actual signature and be on high-quality stationery.

✓ Follow-up calls should be made by the highest-level board or staff member possible. Make sure the person calling is informed about the donor's history with the organization and can speak off-the-cuff. While they should have talking points they can reference, the call should never sound staged.

✓ Make sure that any communication with them provides you additional information on how to keep them engaged with your organization.

Giving Club Revamp Emphasizes Long-Term Intent

When a major fundraising tool is not as effective as it could be, consider retooling it.

Andrea Meloan, director of the Jewell Fund, William Jewell College (Liberty, MO) says their previous leadership giving society was not as effective as they would have liked. "Donors seemed too focused on the first-time member benefit (a name-inscribed brick installed in the Quadrangle, a main part of campus), and we had more lapsed leadership-level donors than we were comfortable with," Meloan says.

Development staff recognized the need for a new society that better emphasized the importance of leadership gifts to the college's annual fund over the long term — and the John Priest Greene Society was born.

This new society honors the legacy of Jewell's longest-serving president, with an eye towards getting donors to make long-term commitments to the college as well. Meloan says the goal is to increase the number of donors who give at the leadership level on an annual basis. "New members join the society after they make a multi-year commitment or a sustaining (until further notice) commitment to the Jewell Fund."

John Priest Greene Society members are expected to make an annual leadership gift of at least $1,000 to the Jewell Fund, at any point during the college's fiscal year. They also refer prospective students, promote the mission of the college in their communities and encourage others to support Jewell in similar ways.

Members receive a members-only quarterly newsletter from the president, an invitation to an annual president's reception and recognition in the annual Honor Roll of Donors report. First-time leadership level donors still receive the inscribed brick on the Quad, which becomes a permanent part of Jewell — something Meloan says she hopes the donor will become too. "We worked to come up with a name for the society that would reflect what this group of people represents for the college — service and support that will have a lasting effect on strengthening Jewell for future generations."

Source: Andrea Meloan, Director of the Jewell Fund, William Jewell College, Liberty, MO. Phone (816) 415-7831. E-mail: meloana@william.jewell.edu

Steps to Kick Off New Gift Club

When development staff at William Jewell College (Liberty, MO) decided to replace an existing leadership giving society with one that focused on donors' long-term commitment to leadership gifts, they knew they had their work cut out for them. Here's a look at their efforts to make the new club successful, by the numbers, six months into the process:

✓ Sent personal invitations to join from the college's president to a select group of 700 people.

✓ Had personal contacts with more than 300 recipients of the invitation.

✓ Sent the first issue of a quarterly newsletter that focuses on affirming how members' annual investments benefit the college.

✓ Have had 20 member households give at the leadership level this year, but have not yet committed to long-term giving.

✓ Have had 10 persons give at the leadership level this year, but decline membership because they could not commit to long-term giving.

✓ Confirmed 100 new members (households) to date, more than half way to their first-year goal of 150.

HIGH-DOLLAR GIFT CLUBS AND GIVING SOCIETIES

Draw More Major Donors With Upper-level Membership Perks

How does an organization ensure that upper-level memberships ($1,000 per year and up) are attractive to individuals of means? By providing at least one of three things, says Lauren Davidson, individual giving manager at the Contemporary Jewish Museum (CJM) of San Francisco, CA: access, recognition or opportunities for socialization.

Museum benefits offering access include priority admission, curator-led tours and invitations to exclusive receptions and artist events. Recognition-based benefits include an annual donor wall, newsletter mention and the option to underwrite major exhibitions and programs.

Benefits providing unique opportunities for socialization often focus on travel opportunities such as a tour of a donor's private glass collection or a tour of featured artists' Bay-area studios.

In offering upper-level benefits, Davidson says, they take into consideration that high-end donors may see the value of benefits differently than persons who give at lesser levels. Davidson takes recognition as an example, noting that the desire for public acknowledgement often wanes at the highest levels of giving.

"People giving $10,000 to one institution are often giving it to several others," she says, "so recognition is not as important to them. We find it generally matters more to those in the $1,000 to $5,000 range because many of them give only to us."

Similarly, Davidson says, when offering social opportunities, museum officials often distinguish between on-site events (generally offered at $1,000 level) and off-site events (offered at $1,800 and up). Doing so, she says, provides a gradation of benefits that encourages individuals to upgrade memberships.

Regarding value benefits such as guest passes and gift shop discounts, she says that when it comes to upper-level donors, "these are not hugely compelling, but they're not meaningless, either," noting that members at the $1,000-plus levels do make use of discounts and special sales.

The most important step to determining benefits that both reward members and encourage them to move up giving levels, she says, is understanding members' fundamental motivation. "We find about 75 percent of higher-level donors are mission-based, rather than benefits-based. The key, then, is structuring benefits to make sure those individuals feel involved with the institution in which they believe. It all comes back to building and strengthening relationships."

Source: Lauren Davidson, Individual Giving Manager, Contemporary Jewish Museum, San Francisco, CA. Phone (415) 655-7829. E-mail: Ldavidson@thecjm.org

---

Strategy Moves Major Donors To Higher Giving Levels

To move individuals to higher (and more profitable) levels of membership, officials at the Contemporary Jewish Museum (San Francisco, CA) rely on a 12-member development committee.

Comprising upper-level members and trustees, this committee offers a range of suggestions on events and benefits and also reviews renewing memberships monthly to decide whom to ask to move to a higher level of membership, says Lauren Davidson, individual giving manager.

Because museum officials have found not asking to be one of the biggest obstacles to development, the majority of members are generally invited to upgrade. Staff at the museum's development office offer background research and coaching if needed, but it is almost always committee members who make the ask.

"These are some pretty savvy fundraisers, and peer-to-peer solicitation has been a very effective tool for us," says Davidson, adding that around a quarter of donors increased their gifts by an average of 80 percent in 2009.